INVITATION
TO
PHYSICAL EDUCATION

INVITATION
TO
PHYSICAL EDUCATION

Hal A. Lawson, PhD

Department of Health, Physical Education, and Recreation
Miami University
Oxford, Ohio

Human Kinetics Publishers, Inc.

Champaign, Illinois

Production Directors
Margery Brandfon
Kathryn Gollin Marshak

Editorial Staff
Dana Finney, Editor
Peg Goyette, Copyeditor

Typesetter
Sandra Meier

Text Layout
Lezli Harris

Cover Design and Layout
Jack Davis

Opening Illustrations
Timothy Stiles

Library of Congress Catalog Number:
83-81454

ISBN:
0-931250-47-1

9 8 7 6 5 4 3 2

Human Kinetics Books
A Division of Human Kinetics Publishers, Inc.
Box 5076, Champaign, IL 61820

1-800-DIAL-HKP
1-800-334-3665 (in Illinois)

CONTENTS

v

ACKNOWLEDGMENTS

No one writes a book without help. I am indebted to sociologist Peter Berger, whose *Invitation to Sociology* illustrated the ways in which an introductory text can be enjoyable and informative; to Rainer Martens for his conviction and vision in calling for a different kind of introductory text; to William Harper for his incisive criticism of an earlier draft of this book; to W. Robert Morford for his continuous support and encouragement; to Dana Finney for her competent and cheerful editing; and to Bonnie Bradshaw for her expert typing. Last, but far from least, Barbara Lawson, also a physical educator, has given me both optimism and realism during times when I needed them. All of these people share any credit that is due for this book.

Sons Michael and Brian have provided the necessary inspiration. I have written the book for them, hoping that their transition from secondary to higher education will be easier than mine was.

H.A.L.
Vancouver, British Columbia, Canada
April, 1983

PREFACE

The textbook is a central feature in North American higher education, perhaps understandably so in societies where education is mass-produced like other commodities. Yet, I have always questioned the extent to which instruction should rely exclusively on a text, and I have criticized most introductory texts for their failure to provide stimulation and substance.

The shoe was on the other foot when I began to plan and write this book. The responsibilities of writing such a book are weighty, because it often is the student's first exposure to physical education. In the face of important questions, the challenge is nearly overwhelming. Who among us claims to have a complete and accurate picture of the rapidly changing profession called physical education? Who would dare to claim mastery over the wide range of knowledge and skills that comprise the field's subject matter? These questions suggest that one of the most exciting features of physical education is also one of the most perplexing for textbook writers: There is now so much to know in physical education, and so many career opportunities, that it is nearly impossible for a textbook like this one to function as an encyclopedia. It can only guide students into the field and place them squarely on the doorstep, with keys in hand, to what physical education can offer them, suggesting at the same time what they can offer to physical education.

With this intent in mind, I have chosen to call this book *Invitation to Physical Education*. Like all good invitations, this one has some prominent features. It spells out some of the details about the field to which the student is being invited. It is structured around the things students are supposed to bring to the field — namely, questions, commitments, and aspirations. In presenting the responsibilities of professionals in physical education, it tells of the student who is invited to the field, and by implication, it tells of the student who is advised to look elsewhere. And finally, it reveals problems and prospects as well as rewards and benefits for those who choose to accept the invitation and who are willing to master the appropriate knowledge, sensitivities, and skills. An introductory text can do little more than this, yet it should not settle for anything less.

A good text should stimulate students at the same time that it informs them. It should encourage them to approach the periodical literature with curiosity and commitment. But none of this will happen if the book is not fun to study, and more importantly, if neither professors nor students are active participants in the process of exploring the profession of physical education. I have tried to spark this process by providing problems and related concepts, not cold, hard facts. My concern is not to provide right and wrong answers, but to frame the important questions. My target is a perspective on the profession, not a catechism.

No textbook is neutral. The writer's biases can always be detected, and this book is no exception. I have tried to compensate for my own biases by providing, at the end of each chapter, a series of study questions and additional readings that students may explore in order to gain a broader perspective on the field. I encourage them to complete these readings and to address the questions in class discussions. I also encourage students to remain mindful of their own questions as they read this book. Ralph Waldo Emerson encouraged readers to make a book their own by writing in the margins while questions and thoughts are fresh. A well read book often is one with extensive writing by the reader as well as by the author. I want this book to bring out the same active responses in its readers.

I am excited about physical education. The field has surely had a significant past, but its greatest contributions can be made in the near future. I hope that this excitement is contagious and that readers will "catch" it as they proceed through the book. To be sure, excitement is not easily communicated via the printed word, suggesting that the total learning experience is as important as this book. Excitement stems from debates about ideas, issues, and prospects. It accompanies the broadening of personal horizons that accompanies good learning. It is derived from personal accomplishment. All of these things should characterize a good introductory course, and this book is aimed in the same direction. That is, the book is a means to this larger end; it is not an end in itself.

So don't spectate on the sidelines. Become an active participant. Catch the excitement of the profession and develop the commitment to share it with others. Such is the appropriate R.S.V.P. for this invitation.

INTRODUCTION
From performer to
professional

Physical education might be called one of the "play professions" because, along with recreation, the substance of its service to society frequently includes forms of play. Virtually every prospective physical educator thrives in the world of play, many having had extensive experience ranging from actually participating, to watching others perform, to reading about play, to teaching and coaching. In fact, it seems fair to say that many students coming into physical education enjoy a love affair with their favorite activities. This is as it should be because physical education by any name is a performance-based field. In other words, the art and science of performance form the heart of the profession's operations.

Yet physical education includes more than personal experiences with performance. One challenge confronting students in the field is that they complement their performance experiences in play with other important kinds of knowledge and skill. The process of learning these things brings with it a personal transition from performer to professional.

Such a transition is not always easy. Research on incoming undergraduate students in higher education has revealed that most have clear-cut views about global issues and about their intended careers. Their world is colored in black and white, and they may resist the notion that things are any other way. Higher education is designed to broaden this narrow frame of mind, replacing one-sided views with a balanced perspective and the capacity for mature insights and judgments. But students often try to protect their "pet" views, setting up a struggle between what higher education is designed to accomplish and what they themselves will permit. This struggle manifests itself in physical education as the transition from performer to professional.

Although all undergraduate students face some sort of transition, it can be argued that students in physical education often have the most difficulty with it. After all, most physical education students have completed years of required physical education in elementary and secondary schools. This experience alone can make quite an impression on them. Each day they viewed first-hand what physical educators did in their work; it was also in this way that they encountered some of the field's subject matter. Moreover, prospective physical educators have decided that physical education teachers are also coaches and that the two responsibilities are very much alike. And finally, students have seen their teachers and coaches remain physically active, perform their work outdoors in nice weather, gain popularity among students and members of the community and, best of all, enjoy long summer vacations.

Little wonder that before they enter college some people believe they are ready to teach physical education and to coach. These rigid perceptions stemming from personal observations are difficult to change, and this is why the transition from performer to professional frequently is most difficult for students of physical education.

Past experiences that shape the choice of physical education as a career are surely valuable, but they are also limiting. Today, more than ever before, opportunities exist to coach, participate, instruct, and counsel in agencies outside the schools—in sports clubs, sport federations, dance companies, body-building programs, health spas, medical clinics, park districts, and the like. The point is, the career opportunities that have opened up in these other agencies require knowledge, sensitivities, and skills that differ in many ways from those displayed in school programs. Furthermore, new ways to teach and coach in schools also are available, suggesting that students have a great deal to learn about their chosen profession of teaching.

So, we can understand how past experiences as a performer and observer often create rigid expectations and perceptions among students entering physical education. This is not to suggest that these perceptions and expectations are entirely wrong, but rather that they usually are incomplete. Neither does this imply that the slate from one's past must be wiped clean, but rather that there is much to learn in higher education that serves to broaden personal horizons while lending new meanings to past experiences. Our discussion continues with these themes, illustrating that students who wish to succeed in physical education and in higher education must learn that their performance mastery and past experience are but a useful beginning in their professional education.

The Limitations of Personal Experiences in Performance

Many students attracted to physical education enjoy helping other people. This motive emerges time and again in studies of recruitment into the physical education major. A typical response to the question of why someone chose physical education is: "I want other people to find the same meaning in physical activity that I have found." This is a noble reason for entering physical education. However, it illustrates the need for a transition from performer to professional, because such a response indicates a bond to personal experience. This personal experience, as indicated next, may provide false leads when it comes to the interests and participation of others.

Common sense dictates that people are alike in some ways, similar in other ways, and yet unique in their own right. So it is with meanings, motives, activity preferences, and participatory styles in physical education. In fact, researchers in physical education have uncovered an array of orientations that people exhibit when they participate in sport, dance, and exercise (Bain, 1979; Kenyon, 1968; Kleinman, 1972). Some participate for a social experience, others for aesthetic reasons, and still others for health and fitness. Whereas some choose high-risk activities for positive stress, others seek the challenges of self-denial that accompany long and rigorous training. Some participate for the recognition and rewards that stem from performance excellence. Others find important meaning in their lives, even in their very identity as persons, through participation. And finally, some seek the sheer fun of playing, often to the point where improved levels of skill are unimportant to them.

Clearly, a variety of meanings, motives, activity preferences, and participatory styles are associated with performance in sport, dance, and exercise. For example, all tennis players are not alike in what they bring to the sport and what they hope to gain from it. In addition, one person may approach the same activity quite differently under different circumstances; the talented basketball player may have one orientation to a championship game and quite another in a pick-up game on the local playground. Furthermore, the same person may shift orientations depending upon the activity; one's approach to golf may differ dramatically from that for swimming.

Thus, human performance in these activities contains nearly as much variety as life itself. Having established this point, let us return to the prospective physical educator who wants other people to find the *same* meanings or motives that he or she has found. Was this person's goal appropriate?

The answer should be apparent: One's personal experience in performance is not always a valid indicator of what *is* or *should be* the experience of others. Recognition and acceptance of this fact is a beginning in the transition from performer to professional. It alerts prospective physical educators to what they need to learn about performance in the years ahead, learning that should complement personal experiences as a performer. Only when a broad understanding of human performance is gained can students hope to prescribe intelligently for other people.

In short, such a broad understanding of human involvement in sport, dance, exercise, and the like is an important safeguard for professional physical educators. It prevents them from forcing their own meanings, motives, preferences, and styles on other people, a process that threatens to strip from these people the very reasons for their attraction to the activity in the first place. This surely would be counterproductive because it could cause people to avoid physical education and participation when the profession's goal is to encourage both.

So unless students make the transition from performer to professional, there are few guarantees that they will properly serve society. Reliance upon personal experiences in performance simply will not suffice for a professional physical educator. Reasoned decision-making also requires new knowledge, sensitivities, and skills that are part of undergraduate education. The rule of thumb then becomes simple: What is known about the activity and the people attracted to it determines what a professional will attempt in the name of service to others.

This procedure appears simple enough, but the foundation needed for reasoned decision-making requires years of serious study. Naturally, this is a primary purpose of an undergraduate education with a major in physical education; or, returning to our main theme, it is the process of becoming a professional physical educator.

A Potential Career: Role-taking Versus Role-making

Another part of the transition from performer to professional demands re-evaluation of perceptions and expectations stemming from one's past experience. Based on *your* past experience, do you really know what it takes to become an excellent coach? Or are you certain that the exercise counselor who so influenced your decision to enter physical education was prescribing appropriate exercises? Or, is it safe to assume that because a former teacher behaved a certain way in your classes you should behave the same way when you begin teaching? No doubt questions like these could be raised about every potential career in physical education. The attendant issues invite students to assess the validity of judgments based on their own experiences. Can anyone identify all of the requirements for good work in a given job—or *role*—after only superficial examination?

If you shift your attention to other professions, it becomes clearer that previous experiences as an observer provide only a clue or two about what is involved in becoming a professional. For example, do trips to the doctor's office or time spent in a hospital reveal everything one needs to know about medicine? Do services rendered by a lawyer tell you all you need to know about law? Of course not. In the same vein, it is risky to assume that past experiences as a young observer are valid indicators of everything you will need for a career in physical education.

As another way to approach this issue, let us assume that you have derived a more complete picture of your potential career than is normally possible. Even so, there is reason to suspect that this picture will not remain valid over the course of your career. Why?

Because rapid social change is a constant in today's society. Some people say it is society's most important characteristic. So although you may have a good picture of what your future career looks like now, the inevitable changes in society will force changes in your career role. You must anticipate these changes and accept new knowledge, sensitivities, and skills that are part of undergraduate education that will equip you for future challenges.

The need for this frame of mind is apparent. Assume for a moment that this year's graduate is 22 years old and will retire at age 65. This person will be in the work force for the next 43 years! Now consider what society and physical education looked like 43 years ago and try to appreciate the enormous change that has occurred in that time. And because the *rate* of change itself is accelerating, the past becomes just a conservative indicator for the future.

Thus, students entering physical education with frozen perceptions and expectations may expect to have difficulty with their higher education; even if they receive a degree they may suffer future shock in the years ahead. Here we would distinguish between students who major in physical education with the intent of *taking* a role or job, and those who anticipate *making* a role. The profound difference betwen *role-maker* and *role-taker* also explains the transition from performer to professional, and it merits further discussion.

Persons committed to role-taking have accepted some potentially dangerous assumptions, having decided that the roles are currently defined and performed in the *best way*. In the process, they have assumed that change is not a constant and that their personal experiences are valid indicators for the future. Thus, they attempt to pattern themselves after existing practitioners, with an eye toward fitting into the same mold in the years ahead. As role-takers, they devalue new knowledge, sensitivities, and skills.

By contrast, role-makers recognize that change is a constant and that their own past experiences must be supplemented by new forms of knowledge, sensitivities, and skills. Their intent is not to ridicule the efforts of existing practitioners, but to help move the field of physical education forward by adjusting roles as suggested by new understanding and social change. Role-makers, in brief, accept social and personal change as a way of life in a profession.

Students entering the field may choose between role-taking and role-making. This choice is available throughout a career, but it is most appropriately made during undergraduate education. Persons who choose role-making will gain the most from their program of study. Those who choose role-taking will not see the relevance of much of their undergraduate education; for them, college will be endured, not enjoyed. And, like it or not, the choice between role-making and role-taking has far-reaching consequences that will affect persons outside the field as well as within it. Look ahead 23 years and try to imagine the experiences that people will have with one of today's role-takers and how this same physical educator will affect the images of his or her colleagues! Clearly, the stakes are high when students opt for role-taking.

The Way Ahead

The remainder of this book has been structured to facilitate your transition from performer to professional. This discussion has an obvious bias: It is aimed at persons choosing to be role-makers.

Four major sections comprise this book. The first encompasses two chapters devoted to the meaning of membership in a profession, and the important evolutionary events in the profession of physical education.

The chapters in the second section address the subject matter of physical education. This subject matter, it is suggested, includes performance experiences, formal knowledge about performance, and the knowledge and skills necessary for work performance in the profession. How this view of the field's subject matter has altered the missions of physical education and opened up new career opportunities will also be discussed.

The third section is devoted to analysis of the knowledge system for physical education. After years of hearing professionals say that new knowledge and skills should be used immediately in practice, it is appropriate to examine in detail the reasons why such use may be facilitated, inhibited, or prohibited; attention to the related parts of physical education's knowledge system accomplishes this task.

The fourth section is brief but important, inviting students to imagine the world of tomorrow and how physical education may change with the times. Students are challenged to act, not react, thereby creating the future instead of passively responding to it.

New knowledge, sensitivities, and skills are presented in the following pages, and these are worthy of discussion and mastery. Perhaps more important to the success of the book is whether you develop a broader perspective on physical education that alerts you to the importance of subsequent coursework in the physical education major. If this latter aim is to be achieved, then this book must provide a foundation in which other parts of the undergraduate experience can be suitably anchored and integrated. Good introductory texts and courses are structured to provide such a foundation. Good students work hard to secure it.

Supplementary Activities

Self-testing Exercises

After reading this introduction, you should be able to:

1. Identify the ways in which personal experiences as a performer and as an observer of work are both useful and limiting as one enters a profession;
2. Distinguish between the orientations of role-takers and role-makers;
3. Discuss the consequences of being a role-taker versus a role-maker;
4. Identify briefly the basis of the transition from performer to professional.

Class Activities

1. Compare the motives for, and meanings in, performance that class members have identified. After searching for commonalities and sources of difference, discuss their implications for people who plan to work in the profession of physical education.
2. Complete a class survey on the reasons for majoring in physical education. Then discuss the implications of the patterns of recruitment into physical education revealed in the survey. This survey can be guided by the following questions:
   a. At what age did you decide to choose or try physical education as a career?

b. Did special persons, experiences, or circumstances influence your decision to enter physical education? If so, identify them.

c. Why did you choose physical education? List the reasons, ranking them from the most to the least important.

d. What do you plan to do with a degree in physical education? What do you hope to accomplish in this role?

e. In your view, what must a person know and be able to do to succeed in the career you have in mind? How many of these things have you mastered or acquired already? How many can and should be gained in higher education?

f. Do you plan to commit your life's work to physical education? Why, or why not?

INVITATION
TO
PHYSICAL EDUCATION

PART 1

PART 1

Part 1 has two chapters. They are like bookends, with the first chapter addressing the meaning of membership in a profession, the responsibilities of such membership, and the uniqueness of professional work. In addition, it identifies the requirements for entry into professional education. Finally, the important parts of professional education are introduced.

The second chapter is like a family tree for physical education. It addresses the meaning of physical education and uses this information to trace the origins and early development of physical education as a modern profession. This discussion is historical, but it is not a complete history. Professionalization is the theme for the discussion, and in this sense there is a direct connection between chapter 2 and chapter 1.

Together the two chapters provide a foundation, showing readers where the profession has been and identifying its important responsibilities and challenges. This is essential subject matter for prospective professionals in physical education.

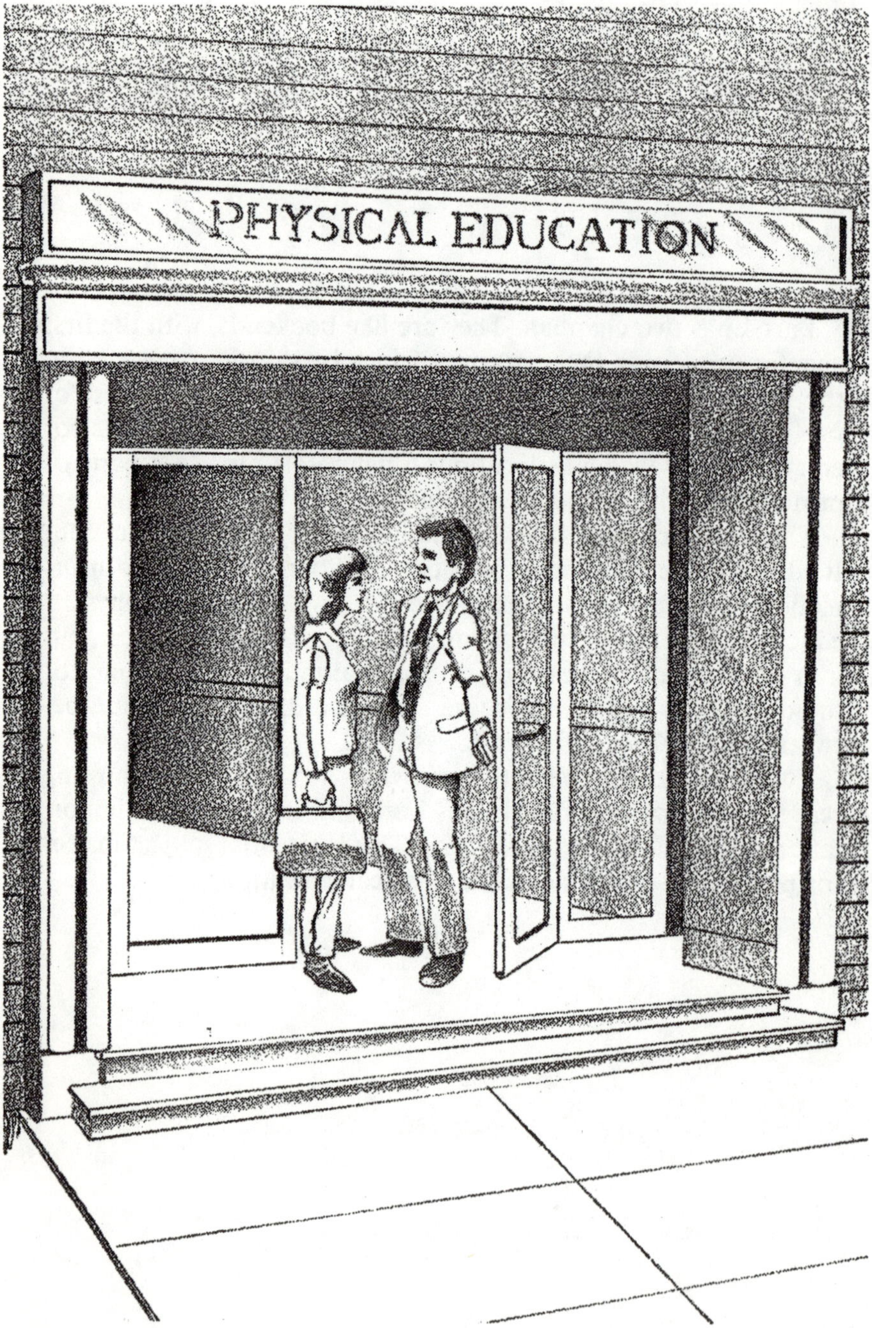
PHYSICAL EDUCATION

CHAPTER 1
Membership in the profession

Your exploration of the physical education profession begins here. This intellectual journey must be thorough, for it may determine both your course of study in higher education and your career. In short, the understanding of the profession that you gain through this discussion and related experiences will influence your decision to accept or reject an invitation to physical education.

It was established in the introduction that you and other newcomers to physical education must make the transition from performer to professional, but what this involves was not specified. If the meaning and responsibilities of membership in the profession were not explained, then there would be a risk of having as many perceptions of the field as there are members. So, the first order of business is to analyze membership in the profession, beginning with the meanings of commonly used terms such as "professional" and "profession."

Athletes, plumbers, doctors, carpenters, and teachers all call themselves professionals. Most of these workers probably are professionals in the sense that their work earns them a living, and many are conscientious in performing it. However, belonging to a profession involves a lot more than working full-time, being paid, and showing concern for the quality of one's work. Thus, the word "profession" is one that many people use but few really understand. Your first challenge is to learn to discriminate—to make judgments about meanings that lie beneath the surface of words like "profession." For just as you often see differences between what individuals say about themselves and what they actually are, so will you encounter differences between what a group of workers calls itself and the extent to which this group is actually a profession.

How does physical education fit into this picture? The term "profession" is used liberally in our literature and our conversations about ourselves. But we must look beneath the surface to learn how valid these uses of "profession" are. Some probing questions can help us. For example, how does work done by a physical education professional differ from work done by a nonprofessional? By what process does a group of workers become a profession? What requirements and responsibilities does professional status demand of individual members? What is the relationship between a profession and members of society? What are the benefits of membership in a profession? How should a newcomer in physical education be prepared for membership in a profession? These questions, important to everyone in a profession, must be analyzed in depth as one contemplates a career in physical education. With these questions in mind, let's begin with an explanation of what will be expected of you as a professional.

Profession, Professionalism, and Professionalization

Have you entered higher education to "get a job," or are you seeking to build a *career*? Your decision will have an impact on the way you approach your studies, the persons you choose as associates, and what your future lifestyle will be like. Furthermore, at the heart of this difference between job and career are divergent commitments to work and equally divergent ways of thinking and behaving in work. These same differences distinguish membership in an occupation from that in a profession. Professionals are committed to one career, whereas other workers may take and leave various jobs. Building a positive commitment toward your career choice now is therefore vital to your status as a professional.

With these points in mind, we can further distinguish a profession from other occupations. We say that all full-time workers are engaged in some kind of occupation, "occupation" being a general term for all kinds of workers. In this sense, a profession is a kind of occupation, but not all occupations are professions. A *profession* is an elite kind of occupation. In contrast with other kinds of workers, its members gain higher status and rewards, often find their work to be more meaningful, frequently enjoy greater control over their work, and usually commit themselves to their careers. "Profession" applies to a special group of workers, such as those in physical education.

In simplest terms, then, a *professional* is a member of a profession. Professionals are committed to the service of others; in fact, it is characteristic of professionals to place the needs, interests, and aspirations of the persons they serve above their own. In addition, professionals conduct research to guide and enlighten their field; similarly, they consult with other professionals to stay current. In this regard, the way professionals perform their work differs dramatically from the way other kinds of workers do their jobs. For example, many kinds of workers rely on trial and error methods in doing their work. Others perform their work without questioning it because it has always been done that way. This dependence on trial and error or tradition is characteristic of occupations called crafts (Morford, 1972).

Thus, professionals differ from occupational workers because knowledge about the substance of the service provided (e.g., sport, dance, and exercise) and about the people served (e.g., students, athletes) determines how they perform their work. Moreover, because knowledge changes along with social change, professionals are able to adapt or alter the way they work. In order to have this flexibility in their work, professionals must master a body of knowledge, sensitivities, and skills enabling them to address ideally the demands of their work. The extent to which individuals live up to these ideals is an indicator of their *professionalism*—a term describing how much an individual upholds the standards of the profession.

The suffix *ization* means "the process of," so professionalization refers to the process by which an occupation becomes a profession. Professionalization is especially fascinating because it involves the relationship of professionals to their society. Indeed, society's members grant a profession its specialized status, and they do so only when the profession has established a good and proper relationship with them. In other words, they judge an occupation's suitability for becoming a profession based on the importance and quality of the services it provides.

To return to an important point, workers can claim to be a profession, but this claim is empty if some important conditions and requirements are absent. The profession must be committed to service. It must have developed a body of knowledge through research, and this knowledge must be used to improve the quality of practice. These are the distinctive features of work in a profession; in fact, they are the core characteristics of a profession because they allow the group to begin to professionalize. These same characteristics—the pledge to service and the uses of research—suggest to society's members that the profession is special and merits their trust.

Another reason society's members grant elite status to a profession is that the problems it addresses in the name of service are seen as important. It is one thing for physical educators to acknowledge the importance of sport, dance, and exercise, but it is quite another for citizens to attach the same importance to these activities. Furthermore, not only must play forms be important to people, but people must perceive the need for expert advice and assistance in learning such techniques. This is why a professional must use research to guide practice—after all, the professional is considered an expert because he or she has mastered the research literature. Most people see this research as too extensive for them to master but they acknowledge an obvious need for its use in practice. Consequently, they grant members of a profession the right to serve them in this capacity.

To summarize, society's members grant professional status because they believe in the importance of the service and the problem(s) the profession addresses (e.g., personal health, worthy use of leisure), and because they identify a personal need for expert assistance. A group of workers can become more or less professionalized depending on how far they have progressed in meeting the requirements and conditions discussed. Some groups are therefore more professionalized than others.

Doctors and lawyers, for example, are considered true or full professionals because they have met all of the requirements and their work is special as a result. These professionals enjoy *autonomy* in their work: They are able to determine what they want to accomplish and the way they want to accomplish it. They

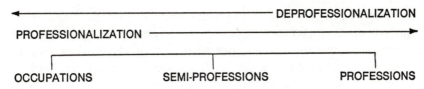

Figure 1. Professionalization and deprofessionalization.

enjoy a *monopoly* as well; persons other than doctors and lawyers would not dare try to perform this work. Doctors and lawyers also receive *high status* and attractive financial rewards for their work. These features of their work tell us that doctors and lawyers enjoy full professional status.

Other groups of professionals do not satisfy completely all the conditions and requirements for professionalization, and as a consequence they do not enjoy the same autonomy, monopoly, and high status in their work.

For example, the physical education teacher often is given a curriculum to teach; this person has less autonomy than do doctors and lawyers, who personally plan their work. Furthermore, people other than physical educators may coach athletic teams both inside and outside the public schools, suggesting that physical educators do not yet enjoy a monopoly over their work. And not every physical educator enjoys the same high status that doctors and lawyers do, although some members of our profession are exceptions. In short, some occupations including those in physical education are more professionalized than most other occupations, yet not as professionalized as the true professions of medicine and law. These are termed *semiprofessions* (Etzioni, 1969), or *minor professions* (Glaser, 1974). Teachers, nurses, and social workers are among the occupational groups in this category.

Thus it is possible to think of a continuum with all occupations at one end, the full professions at the other, and the semiprofessions somewhere in between. Once you begin to think this way, you can chart the ever-changing status of your own profession and others as they try to improve their position in society.

Deprofessionalization

Professionalization is a continuous process because, once achieved, professional or semiprofessional status lasts only as long as society's members see fit to grant it. The very conditions and requirements that allowed the profession to emerge in the first place must be maintained. This is not as easy as it might seem. Sometimes the substance of the service (e.g., sport) may no longer be as important to people as it once was, or sometimes the problems and needs that were once thought worthy of expert assistance are no longer considered so. People also may lose confidence in the experts and begin trying to help themselves. These situations are seeds for reversing professionalization to the point of *deprofessionalization*, the process by which a profession's standing is eroded. Because it gives a profession's members fewer opportunities to perform their work, it is very important that you thoroughly understand the process of deprofessionalization and identify ways to avoid it.

Deprofessionalization has been singled out as an important social change in modern society (Haug, 1975; Toren, 1975), with three related factors contributing to its presence. First, people are more educated today than ever before, and consequently, the knowledge and skills that were once the domain of professionals are now being mastered by other lay persons. For example, physical education programs now offer to everyone some forms of knowledge and skill that only a few decades ago were limited to undergraduate majors in physical education. As a consequence, there is less need for individuals to seek out "the coach" to learn how they might develop a slimmer waistline or improve their tennis serve.

Second, rapid advances in technology have made it possible for people to learn skills without professional teaching. For example, a series of visual aids including film loops, video cassettes, cable television, and computerized machines make it possible for individuals to acquire sports skills just by imitating the action they've watched. They no longer have to rely exclusively upon a teacher or coach for instruction. Even more significant is that instruction can now be at the convenience of the individuals, who can pursue the activity of their choice *when*, *how*, and *where* they want to perform it. Just a few decades ago such opportunities were rare. In this sense, technological advances have served as a basis for deprofessionalization.

In addition, dissatisfaction with professions has prompted some people to begin helping themselves, a trend called the self-help movement. When people begin to help themselves, they initiate deprofessionalization. After all, professionalization thrives on people's willingness to be dependent on a profession; when they become independent, they have less need for the service and begin assigning less status to the profession. This self-help movement is fueled by the fact that today's citizens are well educated and well read, the ever-multiplying list of books and magazines contributing greatly to the growth of the self-help movement. Today, one can even buy kits for divorces and treatment of illness, areas previously reserved for doctors and lawyers. Physical education itself has seen a virtual explosion of popular literature about physical education and sport, much of it written by individuals with no formal background in physical education! In addition, many unqualified persons conduct community classes in exercise and sport; individuals who participate in these classes are helping themselves without expert assistance.

The process of deprofessionalization challenges physical educators to reconsider their fundamental missions and their abilities to solve problems for society's members. The profession must be prepared to change with the times by using its new knowledge and skills to anticipate social change. The profession must be considered important, but more than that, it must be seen as unique. The stakes are high because, as noted earlier, deprofessionalization carries with it a loss of employment opportunities. If physical education is to survive as a profession, it will have to keep changing in order to serve changing members of a changing society.

Returning to a distinction made in the introduction to this book, role-takers have little hope of helping colleagues make the necessary adjustments, let alone make the adjustments themselves. Role-makers, by contrast, anticipate the need for such changes and then work to make them happen. Of course, the ability to anticipate and implement change is only possible for those with a firm grip on physical education's wealth of knowledge, sensitivities, and skills. One earns this background through investments made early in professional education — investments that pay dividends later when one faces the challenges of deprofessionalization.

Education for Membership in a Profession

In professions such as medicine and law, professional education begins after completing undergraduate education, but in others such as physical education it begins at the undergraduate level. However, both systems share common ingredients that are best represented by the question: What will you need to learn in order to become a professional?

Liberal Education

The college or university graduate has responsibilities as a citizen in addition to those as a professional. All citizens must be capable of making reasoned judgments if democracy is to work. A liberal education prepares students for their responsibilities as citizens and helps make possible an enriched lifestyle. The undergraduate physical education major makes important contributions in both areas (Morford & Lawson, 1978). Why, then, you may ask, must I take math (or science, history, etc.)? The answer is, having an undergraduate degree requires the breadth of understanding needed for intelligent citizenship in addition to the depth required for a specific career in physical education. Furthermore, many subjects outside physical education are prerequisites for the mastery of our subject matter.

What *is* a liberally educated person? How would you know whether you were becoming liberally educated? Look for six characteristics or competencies that, upon inspection, should make it clear how subjects outside your field as well as experiences within it contribute to a liberal education.

1. Liberally educated persons know how to acquire knowledge and how to use it.
2. They possess a high level of mastery over the skills of communication.
3. They hold personal values and value commitments but acknowledge that other persons and other cultures hold contrasting values that must be understood and respected.
4. They cooperate and collaborate with others in studying, analyzing, and attempting to solve problems.
5. They are aware of, concerned about, and accept some responsibility for current events and their implications.
6. They continually seek coherence and unity in accumulating knowledge and experience, using the insights thus achieved to fulfill their obligations as responsible citizens in a democratic society (Dressel, 1979, p. 319).

These characteristics and competencies of liberally educated persons are consistent with what has been stated about professionals. Indeed, if professionals are to be effective they must have command over these very same skills and knowledge. Thus, liberal and professional education are fully compatible and even symbiotic; liberal education enhances professional education and vice versa.

Knowledge about Human Involvement in Sport, Dance, and Exercise

You have learned that professionals must have a thorough understanding about the substance of their service and how this service relates to the needs, interests, and aspirations of the general public. In physical education, this applies to knowledge about human involvement in sport, dance, and exercise. Why do people get involved in these activities? What are the consequences of their participation? Are negative outcomes associated with these experiences in addition to the recognized benefits? Such questions point to a need to understand the activities, the people drawn to them, and the consequences of the interactions between these people and their activities.

Before we look at the extent and the richness of this body of knowledge in physical education, let us consider the two ways of acquiring it. First, we learn by actually becoming involved in these activities because there is no substitute for direct exposure. And, we learn by analyzing our personal performance and that of others in classrooms, laboratories, and gymnasia in order to gain the insight that complements our first way of learning—involvement. Thus, we combine the experience of actually performing with an analysis of that performance. The resulting integrated body of knowledge may then be applied in practice.

Professional Skills

Physical educators put their knowledge into practice through professional skills. Their personal performance skills in some sports may be impressive, but they must acquire professional skills beyond what they personally are good at doing. For example, physical educators may orchestrate the development of performance skills in their students even though they themselves may not have these skills. This method may not be ideal for teaching skills but it does suggest that there are professional skills to be mastered in addition to performance skills. For example, special skills of diagnosis, prescription, and evaluation are equally applicable to exercise leaders, coaches, administrators, and prospective teachers. These skills allow the professional to proceed efficiently and systematically in matching the service (e.g., sport, dance) with the people who seek it in order to achieve some intended effect (e.g., health, recreation).

A Professional Ideology

Professional education emphasizes ideology in addition to knowledge and skills. An ideology is an interconnected set of beliefs and values about important concerns such as the ideal person, the ideal society, and the behaviors signifying a life properly lived. Our *professional ideology* encompasses our beliefs about the importance of our work in creating individual and societal betterment. Our sense of mission, and the platform statements we make about physically active lifestyles, are direct expressions of this professional ideology.

A professional ideology grows out of a number of sources, including one's personal experiences and beliefs before entering higher education. Other members of the profession also contribute to the development of an ideology. And some of your own ideology may be drawn from the field's literature, including this book. As you read what others have written, you will find points of agreement and disagreement; in both cases your own ideology is formed and clarified.

How might you now become aware of your own ideology? Record your answers to the following questions: Why am I considering a career in physical education? What is its worth or importance in modern society? How would people and society be worse off if everything about physical education were eliminated? Your immediate answers to these questions are the roots of a professional ideology. By the time you have completed your professional education, a more elaborate and sophisticated set of justifications—which together constitute a professional ideology—will be yours. Although this ideology will be somewhat unique, its common features will unite you with other members of the profession.

Professional Sensitivities

The kinds of sensitivities you must develop during the course of your professional education are most difficult to put into words. These sensitivities, or professional attitudes, are easier to infer from the actions or inactions of professionals in their work. This observation of the nature of professional sensitivities become clarified with two examples.

One important sensitivity a physical education professional needs is a respect for the array of motives and meanings that individuals find in sport, exercise, and dance. Furthermore, the professional must be willing to cultivate these meanings and motives rather than change them; they must be sensitive to differences among individuals and the ways these differences are manifested in activity preferences and participation. Not everyone wants to be an elite athlete. Nor can they be. A sensitive professional therefore tailors services to each client.

A second and related sensitivity also concerns the differences among people. Only rarely can professionals choose their clients. Usually they are greeted by people of all kinds, but good professionals willingly accept this fact. A brief consideration of some of these differences attests to the need for such a sensitivity.

Of course, clients differ in their skin color, gender, age, religious affiliation, prior experience, and native abilities. Furthermore, some do not have complete control over their limbs or their speech and hearing. And clients differ in body builds. It is nearly inevitable that you will encounter these differences in your future work. Rather than allowing these differences to prejudice your thoughts and actions, consider them to be all in a day's work. They illustrate the variety you'll find in working with other people.

In brief, professional sensitivities begin with accepting people as they are, yet caring about what they can become. These sensitivities also reflect your willingness to listen and to accept constructive criticism from the people you serve. Although you may develop these sensitivities during your professional education, the task of maintaining them will span your entire career.

Summary

Membership in a profession carries with it some weighty responsibilities. Not only are professionals expected to commit themselves to a career that involves service, but they also must elevate the needs, interests, and aspirations of others above their own. In addition, the work that a physical education professional does is guided by research. Individual physical educators who fulfill all of these responsibilities demonstrate high standards of professionalism.

The profession of physical education enjoys its status thanks to society's members. The process of professionalization becomes possible when the substance of the service, the problems solved by it, and the professionals' expertise are endorsed by society. When any of these conditions change, professional status is eroded and deprofessionalization begins. Thus, members of a profession must use their knowledge to effect change in their work roles whenever necessary.

The gateway to membership in the profession of physical education is professional education. It is here that you acquire knowledge about human involvement in sport, exercise, and dance. Of equal importance are the other three parts of professional education—professional skills, a professional ideology, and professional sensitivities. Together with the liberal education attained in higher education, professional values, sensitivities, and skills help define the uniqueness of a professional physical educator.

Enhanced professional status should not be the only reason for seeking such uniqueness; rather it should serve to insure quality in the work that is performed. Appropriate professional education and high professional standards in physical education are in the best interests of all of society's members.

Supplementary Activities

Self-testing Exercises

After reading chapter 1, you should be able to:

1. Identify the differences between occupations and professions;
2. Identify the special features of professional work;
3. Distinguish between profession, professional, professionalism, and professionalization;
4. Identify features of modern life that contribute to deprofessionalization in physical education;
5. Identify parts of professional education.

Discussion Questions

1. Is physical education a profession? Why, or why not? What are the implications of your answer?
2. Is there more to physical education than teaching and coaching in the schools? Explain.
3. Are people who work with sport and exercise outside the schools members of the profession of physical education, or members of the profession of recreation? Explain. What are the consequences of your answer?
4. Review the parts of professional education. Are some more important than others? Why, or why not? Is there an ideal sequencing for these parts? In how many of these areas do you feel you have already acquired some preparation? Explain.
5. Is it desirable for people in physical education to use research in practice? Is it possible? Explain.

Class Activities

1. Interview students outside physical education as well as people who are not involved in higher education. Ask for their meanings of the term professional. Ask them as well for their view on physical education. Is work in physical education guided by research? Are physical educators members of a profession? Is this important work?
2. Discuss the ways in which physical educators might combat the process of deprofessionalization. Is there a threat to the very survival of the profession?

For Additional Reading

MORFORD, W.R. Toward a profession, not a craft. *Quest*, 1972, **18**, 88-93.

LAWSON, H.A. Paths toward professionalization. *Quest*, 1979, **31**(2), 231-243.

BROEKHOFF, J. Physical education as a profession. *Quest*, 1979, **31**(2), 244-254.

CHAPTER 2
The emergence of a
modern profession

A profession, like a family, contributes to the identity of its members. This is especially true in North America where one of the first questions we ask a new acquaintance is "What do you do for a living?" This question alone reveals that career and personal identity are intertwined.

For a professional in physical education, then, knowing about this field's roots and early development is nearly as important as knowing about one's family tree. In both cases a person develops a sense of identity and purpose in relation to the knowledge gained. Because entire courses and books are devoted to the history of physical education and/or sport, there is no reason to duplicate such efforts here. Instead, you will be introduced to the profession of physical education—an introduction that discusses important evolutionary events around the theme of professionalization.

What is Physical Education?

The rest of this book is based on the premises that you understand what a profession is as well as the elements of professionalization, and that you understand what "physical education" really means. This book began with a discussion of professions and professionalization in the last chapter, and later will describe the steps involved in the process of professionalization.

For now, let's address two basic questions: What is physical education? From what did it evolve and why? Let's start with a basic definition, treating the term "physical education" as if we were encountering it for the first time. As with defining any new term, the first step should be to consult an unabridged dictionary, which provides not only contemporary meanings but the roots of a term as well. Rootwords suggest clues about a word's history— where it originated and how its meaning has evolved over time. This study of a word and its roots is called an etymology.

In *Funk and Wagnall's Standard Dictionary*, physical education is defined variously as "instruction in the exercise, care, and hygiene of the human body; especially a course in gymnastics, athletics, etc. as in a school or college." This is not revolutionary information, of course, but it does validate common misconceptions about physical education. That is, if you never read past this definition you might believe, as others do, that physical education, play, games, sport, dance, and exercise are all the same. This is a false conclusion, however.

The Funk and Wagnalls' dictionary offers no derivations, or roots, for the term "physical education." This is noteworthy because the absence of roots for the descriptor signals that it is a *modern* construct, that it has gained currency only recently in the English language. This implies that physical education is not as old or as universal as some of the professional literature might suggest. Once again, however, one must be careful in drawing conclusions based on how things look on the surface.

In the first place, it would be wrong to conclude that there were no counterparts to modern physical education in other societies during earlier centuries. There were. These historic programs shared with modern physical education a concern for the human body, performance skills, human expression through movement, or some combination of these things. Furthermore, the educational institutions often sponsored such activities. Beyond these characteristics, however, each of these programs must be viewed as somewhat if not largely unique.

In contrast to today, these societies did not call such activities physical education. There also were different contents, goals, and modes of conduct for these counterparts to modern physical education. After all, the living conditions and cultural climate in early Greece, Rome, Japan, Sweden, and Germany—to name just a few places—differed dramatically from our modern society. In this light, programs of the past have meaning largely in relation to their own time in history and the social circumstances surrounding them. Modern physical education therefore should not be viewed as an inevitable result of other peoples' experiences in quite different societies throughout history. Like these other programs, modern physical education has meaning in relation to the social context and historical period in which it exists—here and now.

Moreover, play, games, contests, sport, and exercise are different from each other and from physical education. Compare play and contests, for example, and you will find that each has its own characteristics. Furthermore, each has its own life and history and each exists apart from physical education programs in schools and colleges. Let's continue this line of reasoning and examine play more closely.

Play has many operational definitions but the term stems from the same root, *plegan*, an Anglo-Saxon word. This root originally meant to bestir oneself, to take a role or pledge, or to be active. Modern usage of play stems from these root meanings (Caillois, 1961; Huizinga, 1955). Play is a voluntary activity with uncertain and economically unproductive results; it takes place in special areas or spaces, often at distinctive times, and its occurrence is often decided by a society's norms.

Because it exists apart from those times and activities that are necessary for survival, play is surrounded by a cloud of make-believe. Perhaps most important of all, the activity itself as well as the conditions surrounding it are controlled by the player. Play is like freedom in the sense that the player feels no constraints (after Gruneau, 1981).

Play and school physical education therefore are not the same, although they may share some common elements. Physical education is required, whereas play is voluntary. Physical education is limited by the fact that it is a school subject, but play cannot be so constrained. The learning outcomes for physical education reveal that it is product-oriented, whereas play is unproductive. These differences cannot be easily dismissed.

On the other hand, there are some important connections between play and physical education. A person's physical education may be worthwhile *preparation* for a form of play. It may even include activities that under different circumstances would fit our definition of play. For example, compare a required class in badminton for grades, credit, physical fitness, and other objectives with badminton freely initiated outside the school: The second situation is more like play whereas the first violates many of play's essential characteristics. Nevertheless, the pathways of play and physical education have crossed and one may have provided preparation for the other.

Many authors have written extensively about the similarities and differences of games, contests, dance, exercise, and sport (Avedon & Sutton-Smith, 1971; Caillois, 1961; Loy, 1972). It is worthwhile to examine the nature of these activities because physical education programs use them to achieve educational purposes. Thus, our examination of how physical education has evolved must include an analysis of why these forms are part of the subject matter and how professionals use them to reach educational goals. Equally important is knowing how such professionals are prepared to teach this diverse subject matter and how physical educators gained professional status. To begin, let's look back at some events that shaped our modern profession.

The Professionalization of Physical Educators

From 1880 to 1920, physical education rose as a profession along with such professions as social work, public administration, and educational administration. These professions both reflected and fueled the emergence of a modern, industrial society.

Remember that a profession is a particular group of people offering specialized services with their expertise, claiming that only they are qualified to offer these services. Physical educators at this time were claiming the right to offer their unique service as they emerged as part of the larger societal picture in which other professions were evolving. The Industrial Revolution fostered numerous changes, not the least of which was greater specialization in work. This affected factory workers as well as professionals, as both fell into step toward a more specialized division of labor.

Physical educators appear to have followed the same steps as other professionals in their efforts to professionalize. Based upon Bledstein's (1976) analysis, these steps were: (a) to isolate important parts of human experience; (b) to label these parts of human experience "problems"; (c) to convince members of society that professional definitions of *problems* also represented people's *needs*; (d) to control the work of servicing these needs; and (e) to add scientific knowledge to professional education and practice. Each of these steps will be explained in the following discussion on professionalization of physical educators.

Isolating Important Parts of Human Experience

At the risk of oversimplification, three parts of human experience were ultimately singled out for attention by physical educators—personal health in general, especially bodily health, sport or athletics, and play, particularly the play of young children. These three areas have merged in today's physical education, but such a combination did not occur universally until the 20th century. Physical educators prior to that time tended to have interests in one area more than the others.

A concern for bodily health grew out of a general movement toward total well-being that had been popularized in the 1820s. Calisthenics and certain forms of gymnastics were identified as the best way toward preventive medicine and bodily health, as the following examples demonstrate.

Catherine Beecher pioneered calisthenic and rhythmic exercises during the 1830s in a program directed specifically at girls and women. This was no small achievement because exercises were not considered ladylike in those days. Yet Beecher persisted, even publishing a book founded on the belief that appropriate exercise is as important to females as it is to males. Because sociocultural change often takes centuries, the work of individuals like Catherine Beecher stands as a significant historical example of people accomplishing great feats under what appear to be impossible circumstances.

Another trend began in US gymnastics programs in the 1820s. Both Canada and the United States opened their doors to large numbers of European immigrants, who had their own favorite brands of exercise, dance, and gymnastics. Two very famous gymnastic activities originated in Germany and Sweden and, as one might suspect, they were reproduced in North American communities of mostly German and Swedish families. Their popularity did not stop there, however. These programs, or their hybrids, along with the special instructors who became their advocates, spread to schools, community agencies, and 4-year colleges.

In the colleges, these gymnastics and exercises were used for preventive medicine. Indeed, many college professors who supervised these activities were also medical doctors, and they called their programs *medical gymnastics*. Whether in the form of medical gymnastics in higher education or physical training in the schools and community agencies, improved physical efficiency was the target. Any other outcomes, such as an improved disposition or greater work productivity, were considered automatic benefits resulting from a trained body.

Sport and athletic programs assumed greater importance after 1852, when the first intercollegiate contest pitted Harvard against Yale in a test of two rowing crews. Many also saw this as a contest between two universities jockeying for stature, and out of this frame of mind grew the basics for modern college athletics. From this point on, the number of colleges, and later, universities, involved in competition multiplied along with the number of participants and variety of sports included in the competition.

Prior to the 1890s students not only *engaged* in intercollegiate athletics, they also *controlled* them. But the 1890s saw an increasing amount of control go to the faculty both at Yale University and the University of Chicago. In addition, full-time professional coaches and athletic directors joined the faculty as persons who assumed greater control over sport and who emphasized the importance of the proper technique needed to win. This demonstrated that athletic programs in higher education were considered important to these institutions, the alumni, and members of the community as well as to the students. Coaches and athletic directors joined in promoting these programs. By the turn of the century, sports debued in the high schools, complete with coaches and the equivalent of athletic directors. These professionals would later influence the physical education programs and, like the proponents of bodily health, stand as pioneers in the profession of physical education.

Emerging with the perceived importance of sport and concern over bodily health was a third area of human experience that was important to the professionalization of physical educators. This concern was play, in general, especially the play of children and teens. Among the proponents of play were physical educators as well as other professionals and citizens, who united to increase the number and kind of opportunities for play. Their collective efforts have been called the *play movement*. As we will see, this concern for play ultimately became an important stimulus for school physical education programs and also spawned a sister profession, recreation.

Although some leaders in the play movement were later to become physical educators, most came from other walks of life. They began organizing during the 1880s in Boston and their ideals later spread to other cities across the US. These persons were concerned about the negative social effects that crowded cities spawned, such as unhealthy living conditions, crime, and commercial amusements like saloons and gambling houses. They believed this environment would adversely influence the growth and development of young children and teens, the adults of the future. Many advocates of the play movement therefore believed that the very future of society hinged upon their efforts. For them, the conditions in the cities constituted a disease—and play was the cure.

Between 1880 and 1900 these civic leaders believed that simply providing more small parks and playgrounds would serve their ends. Therefore, they concentrated on providing only *opportunities*, in the form of facilities, for play, assuming that play was innate and that children would play properly in these new environments. These leaders later changed their minds. They decided that appropriate supervision and leadership would also be necessary if the youngsters' free time—leisure time—was to be used for positive play rather than crime.

Volunteers initially led and supervised the play activities, but later others were paid to do so. Since many of these salaried people were former athletes, it is not surprising that athletics were among the activities they offered children and teens. Then, a concern over efficient use of public funds led government officials in several cities to construct playgrounds on school property. Their reasoning was sound: Why separate playgrounds and play fields from the schools where children spend so much of their lives? Why duplicate facilities? For that matter, why duplicate personnel? The last question eventually led to the schools' employing more and more of these playground supervisors and leaders, and allotting formal occasions during the school day to play. Such measures reflected the importance of play in human experience, wherein the leaders and supervisors of play joined the personnel for athletics and the proponents of bodily health in forming the foundation for physical education.

Identifying Professional Problems

Professional associations serve their members in many important ways, including the sponsorship of conferences. Historians of physical education have hailed the Boston Conference of 1889 as one of the most important meetings in the history of our profession. There, proponents of various approaches to gymnastics and exercise presented papers identifying the merits of their respective approaches with the central issue of serving human needs. Participants at that conference gained mutual understanding of each others' doctrines, but more significantly, they laid a foundation for cooperative efforts in the future. Where they had once competed against one another's respective systems, they could now cooperate to build a framework to accommodate their different views and approaches (after Weston, 1962).

Such a basis for mutual understanding and cooperation is important in the process of professionalization, and it is the professional association that so frequently makes it possible. The association allows people to compromise on issues that would otherwise cause them to splinter. Compromise brings consensus, and a united front is a must if the public is to respect the profession. Thus, it is significant that such a compromise was approached at the Boston Conference, because it paved the way to a larger consensus among members of the profession. Nevertheless, none of the authors used the term *physical education* at this conference; they spoke instead of physical training, with more concern for personal health than for play and sport.

According to Weston (1962), the American Association for the Advancement of Physical Education (the fledgling professional association) met again in Boston in 1890. It was at this second conference that two leaders in the field, both physicians, presented original papers. Dr. Dudley Sargent asked, "Is the Teaching of Physical Education a Trade or a Profession?" Dr. Luther Halsey Gulick, founder of the famous Springfield YMCA and later the Public School Athletic League in New York City, answered with "Physical Education—A New Profession" (reprinted in Weston, 1962, pp. 145-149). With his now-famous paper Gulick set the stage for the evolution of modern physical education, granting a place for physical training, curative exercises (preventive medicine), and recreational activities (sports, games, and play). He also discussed the outcomes that could be expected from all three kinds of activities and suggested the three were more closely related than many had thought.

Shortly thereafter, sport programs began to explode in popularity — first in higher education and then in secondary schools and urban playgrounds. Although these programs were highly organized and controlled, many people still viewed them as play. Thus came the birth of a compromise between advocates of sport and leaders in the play movement. By the time the Playground Association of America held its first meeting in 1906, sport was as common in the playgrounds of large cities as it was in colleges and universities. Indeed, merging playgrounds with schools reflected and fueled sport's popularity. And later, when members of the profession campaigned for statewide measures requiring school physical education, agents of the Playground and Recreation Association of America were among the most influential of their ranks.

The outgrowth of physical education from then on became increasingly complex. What resulted has been called the accommodation of physical education to sport (Lewis, 1969). That is, programs of physical training, whether gymnastics or exercises, grew into programs of physical education in which sports, dance, and games received equal emphasis. Based on the framework Gulick and his colleagues had developed, physical educators now claimed that sports and games curriculum would have the same results as programs directed toward gymnastics and other forms of exercise. And, it would have two additional features. The curriculum would be viewed as play, which would provide fun, relief from stress and, above all, a moral safeguard against the negative social influences of the city. In addition, a physical education program involving sports and games would serve as a good "feeder" system for highly visible and popular interscholastic and intercollegiate athletic programs. This formula seemed to work. Programs initially were designed for boys, with programs for girls following suit much later in this century.

Thus, physical health, moral character, citizenship, skill, freedom from daily stress, and worthy use of leisure were the central needs identified by the fledgling profession. Physical education would meet these needs and also provide instruction for sports and games, intramurals, and athletics.

School physical education, and the school in general, came to be regarded as vehicles for solving problems in our society. They were supposed to prepare people for life and their efforts fell under the banner of "life adjustment education." To speak of physical education was to talk about the schools and the entire process of education.

From Professional Problems to Societal Need

No matter how strongly physical educators claimed that theirs was a profession, their professionalization would have been impaired had society not acknowledged the importance of those issues they identified and the solutions they proposed. The key to this part of professionalization is convincing people that they need what the profession has to offer. People must agree with the issues as defined by professionals. Thanks to strong campaigning for physical education during 1880-1920, this objective was readily achieved.

The major reason the transition was relatively easy can be traced to the diverse people who helped establish the profession. Medical doctors doubled as physical educators, so the strong influence of medicine supported physical education. Sport programs in schools, communities, and institutions of higher education had tremendous public appeal, making physical education seem not only wholesome but absolutely necessary. Recall, too, that respected civic leaders and members of other professions all became involved in the play movement at a grassroots level. These people didn't need convincing; they already had worked diligently to create and improve programs. In the process, they helped the profession of physical education grow.

In other words, the cultural climate was ripe for offerings of physical educators. There was a new awareness of the needs of people who lived in cities. The need for a healthy body was considered basic because, aside from being a safeguard against disease, a healthy body was believed to give rise to the moral virtues called character. People believed that what they called play—games and sports—were the ideal means of developing a healthy body and, in turn, character. They further believed that through participation in games and sports individuals would acquire those attributes necessary for political order and a good future society. Such participation also exemplified worthy use of leisure time.

In Control of a Professional Service

From this foundation, established in the late 19th and early 20th centuries, came a more visible profession that endeavored to increase control over its offerings. The profession's goal was to improve the professional preparation of its members so that, in proclaiming themselves to be experts, they could demonstrate that they had completed the necessary education and training.

Consequently, as this century progressed, preparation for membership in the profession expanded from short-term courses offered in community agencies to more formal, longer term courses offered in colleges and universities. Indeed, institutions such as Oberlin College and the University of Nebraska were offering 4-year degree programs near the turn of the century. More frequently, however, teachers and coaches for the new profession of physical education received their preparation in institutions called "Normal" schools, which initially had 2-year curricula. Normal schools gradually expanded to 4-year institutions, with degree programs in physical education expanding to 4 years at the same time. Nevertheless, 2 or 4 years of formal, higher education was rare during an era when many people did not complete high school! In a society that assigned increasing value to such formal education, completing 2 or 4 years demonstrated a special kind of expertise for physical educators. Their formal education, and the increasing sophistication of their programs, allowed them to make great strides in gaining control over the problems they had identified.

On the other hand, a familiar problem of today was also apparent in the early 1900s: Highly talented athletes with no formal background in physical education were often taken to be professional physical educators. In short, from the beginning there has been some confusion in people's minds about the difference between a skilled athlete and a professional physical educator. The task was then, and is now, to remove this confusion by introducing scientific and scholarly study into professional preparation.

Enter Science

The mere mention of science conjures up images of research and researchers. There were few researchers and even less research in the beginning, however, because reaching consensus and starting a new profession were challenging enough. And programs of professional preparation were initially geared toward practitioners, not researchers.

Furthermore, early programs of professional education, unlike their counterparts of today, were patterned after existing practices. Dr. Clark Hetherington, often called the father of modern physical education, instituted such a model. He did this for a good reason, however. Emerging school programs abounded, but qualified teachers were in short supply. To solve this problem, Hetherington suggested that professional education programs for prospective physical educators be structured after a "job analysis," in which other professors examined what teachers and coaches did in the schools in order to learn what should be offered as part of the undergraduate degree program in physical education (Bronson, 1958, pp. 101-128).

Walter Kroll (1971), a modern scholar, has summarized the four parts of these early degree programs in physical education: (a) performance skill courses in sports and games; (b) teaching methods and materials courses for these activities; (c) curriculum and administration courses; and (d) courses in the growth and motor development of children (p. 77). Only in the fourth part was science accorded importance.

Beginning with the 1930s, though, more and more physical education professors became interested in research. Initially they tried to apply scientific findings from areas such as education, psychology, and physiology to questions and problems in physical education. Their efforts materialized in textbooks for specialized courses. Called *Principles of Physical Education*, these books and courses served as encyclopedias for physical education and were designed to improve and justify all the operations in physical education, including professional preparation and school practice. These books and courses were supplemented by the few scholarly journals for the field.

From the time the first principles book appeared until the early 1960s, the scope and length of publications grew as the number of researchers and the pace at which they produced results increased. During this time, predictable offshoots of these books were written. For example, special courses were needed in exercise physiology because there was too much material to cover in a principles book.

Research, especially scientific research, had now been added to professional education and practice in an effort by physical educators to professionalize. Once completed, it attested to the maturity of a profession born but a few decades earlier.

Summary

Physical education is a modern invention; likewise, the birth of physical education as a formal profession is a contemporary event. How it emerged in relation to play, games, sport, and forms of gymnastic exercise is intriguing. Even more intriguing are the compromises that had to be made for such a version of physical education to emerge. Its emergence and rapid growth stand as tributes to the pioneers of physical education—people such as Beecher, Sargent, Gulick, and Hetherington—who provided the commitment and insight that stand as early examples of professionalism.

The professionalization of physical educators followed the same steps taken by other professions, the first step being to isolate important parts of human experience (in this instance, bodily health, sport, and play). Once these parts of human experience were identified, the next step was crucial. *Problems* surrounding these segments of experience were translated into human *needs*. In other words, it was one thing for physical educators to identify problems in cities that could be solved by participation in play, games, sport, and exercise; it was quite another to convince people that they all *needed* these activities. This was accomplished. Nevertheless, the process of professionalization was not yet finished.

The next step was to gain *control* over these needs. That is, physical educators had to acquire the authority to dictate how these needs should be met. They had to convince others that the skills and knowledge required to meet their needs were specialized and that they, as physical educators, possessed those special skills and knowledge. Consequently, physical educators established their programs of study in the colleges and universities.

The final step was the addition of science to professional training and practice. Science serves a number of purposes. It yields a special kind of knowledge, reassuring each group that they are elite and deserve special power and authority. Science yields better ways to accomplish the profession's goals, and it is a source of prestige. In short, it is another means by which professionals can answer questions pertaining to the field.

Supplementary Activities

Self-testing Exercises

After reading chapter 2, you should be able to:

1. Identify the differences between play and physical education;
2. Indicate the importance of completing an etymology of a new word;
3. Identify the steps that together comprised the professionalization of physical educators;
4. Discuss the compromises that pioneers in the profession had to make to unite the membership;
5. Describe the platform for the profession that emerged as physical education accommodated to sport;
6. Identify the components in the first programs of teacher education in physical education;
7. Discuss the role of scientists and science in physical education.

Questions for Discussion

1. What are the differences between school physical education and play? Can school programs be designed so that they correspond with play? Is this desirable?
2. In what ways do the conditions of today differ from those when programs of physical education first developed? Is there still a need for school programs? If so, should they remain in their original form? What objectives should they attempt to achieve?
3. Is professionalization a good thing? Has the process of becoming a profession helped physical educators? Has it helped students and the general public? Explain.
4. Was it a good thing for medical doctors to leave the profession of physical education? Why, or why not?
5. Should modern programs of training teachers be any different from their original counterparts? If so, how? Why?
6. Is it appropriate to limit the concept of physical education to the schools? Why, or why not?

Sources for Additional Reading

BOYER, P. *Urban masses and moral order in America, 1820-1920.* Cambridge: Harvard University Press, 1978.

CURTIS, H.S. *The play movement and its significance*. New York: MacMillan, 1917.

CURTIS, H.S. *The practical conduct of play*. New York: MacMillan, 1920.

HOWE, F.C. *The modern city and its problems*. New York: Charles Scribner's Sons, 1915.

LEWIS, G. Adoption of the sport program, 1906-1939: The role of accommodation in the transformation of physical education. *Quest*, 1969, **12**, 34-46.

RAINWATER, C. *The play movement in the United States: A study of community recreation*. Chicago: University of Chicago Press, 1922.

WESTON, A. *The making of American physical education*. New York: Meredith, 1962.

PART 2

Physical education is portrayed in the following chapters as a profession in transition. Nevertheless, its original missions of starting and improving school programs are reinforced and their future importance is acknowledged.

One reason for the rapid changes in physical education is the disciplinary movement; its story is told in chapter 3. Aside from the work of key people, the important events and conditions that facilitated the movement are described. The reasons why some endorsed this movement, whereas others attacked it, are identified.

Chapter 4 discusses the art and science of movement performance. Here, too, are signs of change in the profession as more and more people study human performance in play, games, sport, dance, and exercise. Exemplary findings and important questions are raised in the course of this discussion to make readers reflect on their own experiences.

A profession in transition is bound to have its controversies, and these begin with conflicting concepts of the field's subject matter and missions. Chapter 5 presents a framework for viewing the field's past and future, a framework in which new missions are made possible by new definitions of its subject matter. These transitional features about physical education, with an enduring commitment to school programs, generate excitement about the profession's future.

Chapter 6 is devoted to career planning in physical education. It begins with the framework introduced in the previous chapter and identifies practical ways in which readers may consider career choice and preparation for such a career. Teaching and coaching remain important career possibilities, but a profession in transition has more to offer prospective members. These alternative careers are identified, and readers are shown how to use courses in physical education and related fields to prepare themselves for their future work.

CHAPTER 3
The disciplinary movement

The last chapter traced the beginnings of the modern profession of physical education, identifying the steps involved in the professionalization of physical educators and stressing the importance of compromise and consensus in this process, both then and now. To speak of compromise and consensus, however, is not to deny that differences of opinion exist, particularly concerning the future of the profession. In every profession, there are always those whose opinions differ from the majority's. Indeed, it is possible to encounter several groups of people in a profession, each group forged out of their common opinions; these groups compete against each other for the favor of the majority of the profession's members. As long as one group's vision of the profession and its future is dominant, little visible change occurs. But when another group gains the upper hand, the profession may change. That is, differences of opinion within a profession may lead to new compromises and a new basis for consensus. This is the political reality in a profession. Like politics in general, it requires members to be especially persuasive in advancing their views.

From the beginning of physical education as a profession, differences of opinion have existed and identifiable groups have formed around these opinions, each trying to persuade the others that its vision of the profession is the best. Witness the ever increasing number of researchers in physical education who appeared on the scene in the middle of the 20th century. Foremost among them were the specialists in exercise physiology and motor learning, who had received their undergraduate degrees in physical education but completed some graduate study in other fields. Their visions for physical education were colored by these educational experiences and by their own special interests. Unlike the majority of members early in the profession, these researchers believed there was more to the field than the nearly exclusive emphasis upon school programs and the preparation of teachers. In their view, research was not to be limited to improvement of teaching and school programs, nor should their own courses in higher education have been so limited. They wanted to learn more in their research about exercise and sport in general, and they wanted their courses to reflect this.

Researchers with these views increased steadily in number during the 1950s and early 1960s as graduate programs in physical education multiplied. Events in the middle 1960s created a climate that granted their views new importance both in the profession and in society at large. Indeed, the profession has not been the same since these researchers promoted their visions for physical education. Therefore, these events and the key actors should be examined so that the resultant changes can be better understood.

James Bryant Conant as a Catalyst

By its very presence, a chemical catalyst speeds up a reaction although it may remain unaffected by it. Just as there are chemical catalysts, so too are there social catalysts such as James Bryant Conant, whose work caused reactions and changes in physical education.

A former President of Harvard University, Conant in 1961 began to study teacher training in all fields. Two years later he published the results of his investigation in *The Education of American Teachers*. In it, Conant recommended specific changes, and his findings and recommendations about physical education shook the field.

Conant acknowledged physical education as a school subject with a performance base, but he also pointed out that improvement in motor skill or physical skill through activity courses was considered the only subject matter of physical education. He observed that professors of physical education had an attitude about their subject that was "something like an inferiority complex" (p. 181) and that,

> one consequence of this attitude in the case of art, music, and physical education has been an attempt to gain respectability by adopting the phraseology and symbols characteristic of faculties of arts and letters, such as listing with a course number "Football Fundamentals," "Advanced Basketball," and "Textiles I and II. . . ." All this seems to me a pity. (Conant, 1963, p. 181)

He therefore recommended that all such courses be eliminated and replaced by proficiency examinations. Because he believed that physical education was a performance-based field, Conant thought that skill or proficiency in these activities ought to be *prerequisite* to higher education, not a part of it. He observed,

> And it is obvious that some of the skills in the sports demanded today of the physical education teacher would be manifest in high school. (Conant, 1963, p. 183)

Conant was suggesting that the subject matter of many professional preparation programs in higher education was more appropriately the subject matter for secondary schools! But he also pinpointed "the total youthful experience" as worthy of consideration in determining admission to teacher training programs in physical education (p. 183). He recommended that students without such entry skills be directed to other undergraduate programs and not even be admitted to physical education.

Conant went a step further, recommending that a student in physical education not take a second major or academic concentration. Because he had observed the tendency of physical education teachers to become school principals, he believed that "the physical education teacher should have an even wider, general academic education than any other teacher" (Conant, 1963, pp. 183-186). Here again, the implication was that physical education's subject matter consisted only of "physical skills and applied techniques" (p. 185). Subjects with real academic substance were to be found *outside* the field.

Even today, these opinions and recommendations can be viewed as penetrating criticisms of undergraduate education in the field. Yet Conant directed his most penetrating commentary at graduate education in physical education:

> I am far from impressed by what I have heard and read about graduate work in the field of physical education. If I wished to portray the education of teachers in the worst terms, I should quote from the descriptions of some graduate courses in physical education. To my mind, a university should cancel graduate programs in this area. (Conant, 1963, p. 201)

To be sure, these graduate programs were built logically upon their undergraduate counterparts. And Conant was chipping away at both, at the very foundation of the field. He was suggesting that a unique body of knowledge in physical education did not exist, even though he found clues for such a body of knowledge in what he called "the physiological sciences" (p. 207). Even at the graduate level, the body of knowledge for physical education was physical performance skills and applied techniques, and these did not merit graduate credits.

Physical Educators Respond to Conant's Challenge

The famous historian Arnold Toynbee observed that civilizations develop by responding to successive challenges, remaining healthy as long as they identify these challenges and maintain the capacity to respond to them. The same pattern of challenge and response marks the health of a profession. In light of Conant's challenges, physical educators responded and grew as a consequence.

By the time Conant's book appeared, the traditional program in physical education as conceived by Clark Hetherington already was being altered. Many in the profession are credited with these changes, but most of the credit belongs to the scientists and scholars of a few prestigious universities. These people had whittled away at courses entitled "Principles of Physical Education," creating instead a series of separate and specialized courses in motor learning, exercise physiology, and motor development. "Principles of Physical Education" became, as a consequence, "History and Principles of Physical Education" or "History and

Philosophy of Physical Education." And in both cases the course and its professor became equally specialized. These were important changes in the undergraduate major, and other colleges and universities began to follow suit.

After devoting their attention to the undergraduate program, this same group of professors also altered graduate programs in the field. They assigned a greater role in the latter to theory and research because they envisioned the need for more researchers, the need for professionals to use research in practice, and the need for a body of knowledge for the profession that was broader than its predecessor. These visions reached down to the very foundations of physical education.

Teacher education programs had also begun to change during this same period. Here, too, physical educators had made great strides in upgrading graduate and undergraduate programs. Thus, Conant's criticisms and recommendations affected teacher educators as much as other scientists and scholars in the profession.

Conant's work must be viewed in another light: The professors who tried to improve graduate and undergraduate programs in physical education had to overcome strong resistance within the profession. And no sooner did they experience a small measure of success than they had to confront opposition from outside the field. The stakes were high; physical education's image and role in higher education were on the line.

Many people in the profession readily responded to Conant's challenge. One particularly strong response, from Franklin M. Henry of the University of California, sparks controversy even today and its ultimate impact is undeniable.

Henry responded to Conant's challenge in 1964 in an oral presentation to his colleagues in the National College Physical Education Association. His presentation, published in the *Journal of Health, Physical Education, and Recreation*, was entitled "Physical Education: An Academic Discipline" (Henry, 1964) and remains a classic work.

Although Henry did not name Conant in his response, he targeted Conant's criticism of graduate work and the field's subject matter. The title alone was revealing: An "academic discipline" is usually considered a formally organized body of theoretical and scholarly knowledge that is disseminated to those who choose to master it. Many academic disciplines end in the suffix "-ology" (the study of), such as sociology, psychology, and physiology. So by suggesting in his title that physical education was itself an academic discipline, Henry countered Conant's conclusion that the field's subject matter was limited to physical skills and applied techniques. Henry contended that theoretical and scholarly subject matter did exist in physical education, quite apart from the mission of teaching physical education in educational institutions.

It is only natural that Henry's own position at the University of California would influence his response, for he had done pioneering work in physical education, both in changing curricula and in doing research. He was interested in motor learning and control and worked closely with many of his graduate students who later joined the ranks of physical education's researchers. Henry's academic discipline, then, was a descriptive and prescriptive response to Conant. He was describing and justifying what he and colleagues were already doing and prescribing for others in the field. He said, "If the academic discipline of physical education did not already exist, it would need to be invented" (Henry, 1964, p. 33).

The rest of Henry's response was addressed as much to colleagues in the field as it was to outsiders like Conant. To colleagues in the field, Henry spoke of the need for such a discipline and gave reasons why it had not fully developed. He isolated physical education as having

> the dubious distinction of being a school subject for which colleges and universities prepare teachers but do not recognize as a subject matter field, since the typical physical education department is unique in being under the jurisdiction of, or closely related to, the school or department of education. (Henry, 1964, p. 32)

Henry's meaning becomes clear by analogy. Other prospective teachers studied a parent discipline such as physiology or English, and only later did they consider how to teach this subject matter through courses in education. By contrast, Henry pointed to the student in physical education.

> The student who obtains a bachelor's degree in physical education typically has a major that is evaluated and oriented with respect to what he is to teach in the secondary schools, and how he is to do the teaching or administer the program. Many physical education major programs, for example, do not require a course in exercise physiology. (1964, p. 32)

Henry felt that this difference between physical education teachers and teachers of other subjects resulted from too many professors in physical education being teacher educators whose own experience in schools and graduate education were inappropriate for an academic discipline. That is, the subject matter of teacher education was an example of what an academic discipline was not.

To underline his point, Henry addressed the matter of physical performance skill, which he viewed as a worthy objective in its own right. However, Henry did not view the development of such skill as part of disciplinary study. He suggested that courses for skill, along with rules and strategy for sports, were inappropriate for upper division coursework in a college or university and instead held a place in lower division study. With this, Henry was adopting a middle-of-the-road position in relation to Conant and former practices in physical education.

Concerning Conant's suggestion that students interested in exercise physiology should study in a physiology department, Henry argued that students wanting to learn about exercise and sport could not be accommodated in traditional disciplines such as physiology. He noted that these activities received only peripheral, if any, treatment in the traditional disciplines. He argued further that the academic discipline of physical education was unique and necessary in its own right, and that its subject matter should not be developed by blind borrowing of subject matter from other disciplines. A student's understanding of exercise stress, for example, required him or her to be more than a child of physiology. A comprehensive understanding of exercise stress could only result from the student's ability to cross the boundaries of several, related disciplines, each of which promised understanding of exercise. For Henry, physical education's academic discipline was *cross-disciplinary* because each of its students faced the task of mastering portions of several related disciplines. On these points Henry rested his case.

The Cultural Climate for the Disciplinary Movement

As noted earlier, change in history can always be traced to human actions and reactions. Change in physical education is no exception. Conant's and Henry's pivotal roles as catalyst and reactor are consistent with this observation, yet it is true that changes occur more easily when the conditions are right. This was also the case for the disciplinary movement, a discussion of which must include mention of the cultural climate that was ripe for this change.

During the late 1950s and 1960s, North Americans were witnessing a call to educational essentialism as tremendous pressure was placed upon all educators to emphasize the basics of education, the so-called "essentials." Mathematics and science in particular were accorded the greatest priority because the Soviet Sputnik had triggered an international race in space-age technologies.

At the same time, politicians were concerned about the cost-effectiveness of higher education programs, just as they are today. They examined the colleges and universities in their states and provinces, asking some pointed questions. For example, they questioned why a particular physical education program was being offered on one campus and not another, or how many programs of physical education were needed in higher education. Such questions helped to launch extensive efforts to control the degree programs in higher education.

Consider the implications of such questions for physical education during the late 1950s and early 1960s. Colleges and universities virtually everywhere offered majors in physical education; despite some minor differences, these programs were remarkably alike. Furthermore, there was often duplication *within* the same institution because many had separate departments and programs for men and women. Therefore, when faced with questions about duplication of programs, many physical educators tried to emphasize or create uniqueness in their own programs. Among the first to survey programs in colleges and universities for duplication was the state of California, and it was no mere coincidence that Henry worked at the University of California. Other leaders in the disciplinary movement (Abernathy & Waltz, 1964) were also from that same state.

Thus, the disciplinary movement in physical education resulted from other reasons besides Conant's challenge and Henry's response, as certain cultural factors made the climate ripe for change in a few colleges and universities. Change they did, but not without controversy.

The Disciplinary Movement: Change and Controversy

The disciplinary movement, which began with Henry's response to Conant in 1964, gained momentum during the last part of the decade. This momentum brought questions: What was the subject matter of physical education? Was Henry's discipline part of it? Were physical performance skills part of it? If Henry was correct in calling for a discipline, what was the relationship between it, teaching, and performance activities? Was this to be a discipline *of* physical education, or *for* physical education? What was physical education? Indeed, if physical education was taken to mean a school subject for which colleges and universities prepared teachers, could it also be a discipline that presumably existed apart from applied work? Many of these questions remain unanswered today.

People in the profession asked these questions differently, obtaining answers that were far from uniform. Different groups had their own version of the "real" physical education, each group working to realize its version. The differences among groups were reflected in publications, in the kind of professors hired, and in the design of degree programs for undergraduate and graduate students — all visible signs of rapid and dramatic changes in the profession. These changes served as sources for heated controversy.

Although several diverse groups can be identified, the early controversy surrounding the disciplinary movement is best described by sketching two groups: those in favor of the disciplinary movement who helped usher it along, and those opposed to the movement who took a different direction.

The New Disciplinarians of Physical Education

Just as the founders of the profession of physical education had expressed their views in meetings of the professional association and in the field's literature, so, too, did the proponents of the disciplinary movement. They addressed the subject repeatedly at professional meetings and published their views in the field's journals and books. The skill with which their ideas were disseminated gradually increased, and by the end of the 1960s, proponents of the movement had begun to develop a convincing case that appealed to more and more people in physical education. Soon, an identifiable group of professionals formed because of their implicit consensus on three related goals.

Their first goal was to develop a body of knowledge for the field in the manner that Henry advocated, a body of knowledge that would be gathered and organized without immediate reference to school programs and teaching. Second, however, they shared a concern for the relationship between this discipline and its practical applications such as teaching and performance in sport and exercise. The third concern, implied in the first two, was their goal of including disciplinary knowledge in defining the subject matter for physical education.

Recommendations for other changes followed. New undergraduate and graduate curricula were proposed and implemented as the education and training of professors shifted outside physical education departments. In the process, "new disciplinarians" gained positions on faculties of physical education and they instituted curricular changes.

Some departments accepted the disciplinary emphasis but retained the name physical education. Other departments substituted such labels as "human movement studies" (Abernathy & Waltz, 1964), "physical activity sciences" (Larson, 1965), and "sport studies" (after Sheehan, 1968). *Kinesiology*, a label we shall employ, was a later choice; it stemmed from the Greek word *kine*, meaning movement or motion, and thus means the study of human movement. The debate over names was quite important to the new disciplinarians. In their view, this was a discipline *for* physical education, one that should not be confused with the more common meanings of physical education as a school subject. They were concerned with the study of sport and exercise for its own sake, not with the applied mission of changing and maintaining student behavior. On the other hand, convinced that prospective teachers and coaches should master their subject matter, the new disciplinarians believed that prospective teachers were best housed in what used to be called departments of physical education, along with teacher educators. Not everyone in the profession agreed, however, especially a group of teacher educators.

Opponents to the Disciplinary Movement

Opposition to the disciplinary movement began early and remains formidable even today (Broekhoff, 1982; Siedentop, 1980). Following are some primary reasons why some colleagues were, and are, opposed to the disciplinary platform.

First, not everyone agrees that disciplinary knowledge, as defined by the new disciplinarians, should relate to practice in schools, let alone be essential for it. Likewise, some people do not believe that disciplinary knowledge is part of the profession's subject matter, nor do they consider it indispensable in preparing teachers and coaches. Quite to the contrary, opponents suggest that disciplinary study actually detracts from the business of preparing teachers and coaches and improving school programs. They instead maintain that disciplinary knowledge has no practical application in the schools, and thus it is deemed a frill.

A second point of opposition—equally related to school programs, teachers, and teacher educators—concerns a perceived loss of human resources to the disciplinary camp. That is, opponents suggest that many promising teachers and teacher educators are lured away from their potential roles by disciplinary study (Siedentop, 1980), resulting in less quality in teacher education and school practice. This, of course, alarms them and fuels their opposition to the disciplinary movement.

A third issue concerns the allocation of money, facilities, and equipment in higher education. Prior to the disciplinary movement, most of these resources were automatically funneled into teacher education, but the disciplinary movement has seen a redistribution of these nonhuman resources. Instead of being allotted to teacher education programs, money is used to build and maintain laboratories for research and teaching. Considering that many teacher educators do not even view disciplinary study and the new disciplinarians as part of physical education, one can understand why they oppose the reallocation of resources.

Other opposition stems from disagreement about the proper discipline for physical education. Some teacher educators are not as concerned about whether a discipline is needed in physical education as they are about *which* discipline is appropriate and how it should be defined. Many of them reject a discipline of kinesiology, but accept a discipline organized around the science of teaching and coaching (Broekhoff, 1982; Siedentop, 1980). They call this discipline pedagogy, or sport pedagogy, and consider it every bit as scientific as that proclaimed by Henry. However, an important distinction between the two views of the discipline is implied here: Henry's discipline, you recall, exists apart from application, but sport pedagogy is designed with an eye toward application. That is, pedagogy is supposed to guide practice and its subject matter can be divided into courses comprising teacher education. Thus, opposition centers around different disciplinary frameworks, which in turn stem from different working definitions of a discipline. Furthermore, Henry and the new disciplinarians proclaimed a discipline *for* physical education and gave it a new name, while these teacher educators have called for a discipline *of* physical education—with the *same* name.

A Final Comment

These two opposing groups illustrate how changes accompanying the disciplinary movement have bred controversy. However, recognizing only two groups both oversimplifies and misrepresents the status of the field, and also overlooks the efforts of some colleagues to reconcile these and other divergent views. Perhaps most importantly, it does not capture the genuine excitement that has existed throughout the profession during this change and controversy.

So let's return to Toynbee's notion of challenge and response as applied to the profession, understanding that the mere presence of internal negotiations and debates are a healthy sign for the field. Surely this field, far from being static, is a dynamic one in which the number of questions and challenges generate excitement and enthusiasm. One can even argue that the field is gradually making room for disciplinary study of both kinds as well as professional applications for both, an argument that will be developed in subsequent chapters. For now, let's be optimistic and remain confident that the profession will continue to grow and develop.

Summary

The disciplinary movement emerged in the middle 1960s as an important force in physical education. It stemmed from the efforts of professors in physical education to expand the field's focus from one exclusively concerned with teaching and coaching to one that included all possible parts of exercise, sport, and play. The work of James Bryant Conant served as an important catalyst for this disciplinary movement, which was also enhanced by cultural conditions such as the strong educational essentialism of the 1960s and the efforts to find unique aspects of physical education programs in higher education.

Franklin M. Henry's work to establish a discipline was met with similar efforts by others. Within 10 years, undergraduate and graduate curricula in many institutions had been revised. New faculty members, the "new disciplinarians," conducted research and designed courses in areas not directly related to teaching and coaching in the schools. And, they maintained that their subject matter was foundational and essential for school practice, that theirs was a discipline *for* physical education, not of it. So they replaced "physical education" with names such as kinesiology. In this view of a discipline, knowledge was gained for its own sake and need not have any immediate application to practice.

Opposition to the disciplinary movement, as voiced by many teacher educators, was anchored in a number of related concerns including the loss of human and nonhuman resources to the disciplinarians. These teacher educators questioned whether Henry's discipline was the proper discipline for physical education and, for that matter, whether it had any connection to physical education. They instead proposed a discipline concerned with pedagogy as a discipline *of* physical education, not for it. Debate continues today over which discipline is appropriate for the profession.

Obviously, then, the disciplinary movement has been a source of change and controversy. As with all such change, there is a need for compromise and a new consensus among members of the profession. In this sense, the challenge for the 1980s is much the same as it was for the profession's founders in the 1890s. How these divergent points of view can be merged to serve the profession and society is a question that must be addressed in the first part of an invitation to physical education.

Supplementary Activities

Self-testing Exercises

After reading chapter 3, you should be able to:

1. Identify and describe Conant's objections to the work being conducted in physical education;
2. Describe Henry's view on the academic discipline of physical education;
3. Identify key events and conditions that fueled the disciplinary movement;
4. Indicate points of agreement among those who favored this disciplinary movement;

5. Identify criticisms of this disciplinary movement;
6. Discuss how and why the disciplinary movement created such change and controversy in physical education.

Class Activities

1. Interview students and faculty outside physical education, asking what they think is the subject matter of physical education. Ask them also if they think that an undergraduate degree in physical education is as valuable as degrees from other fields.
2. Discuss the extent to which researchers for Henry's discipline are part of physical education, the profession. Ask other students and faculty in physical education for their views on the matter.

Questions for Discussion

1. What were Conant's primary criticisms of the major in physical education? Do you agree with these criticisms? Do they in any way appear to apply to your own undergraduate major program? How would you counter Conant's arguments?
2. Do you think Henry provided a satisfactory response to Conant?
3. From your perspective, was the development of an academic discipline a blessing, a plague, or a bit of both?
4. What are the potential sources of friction between physical education and kinesiology? In what ways might the two be identical? Complementary?
5. Is it necessary to have separate names for school programs and the academic discipline? Why or why not? Is kinesiology the best name for this discipline?

Sources for Additional Reading

ABERNATHY, R., & Waltz, M. Toward a discipline: First steps first. *Quest*, 1964, **2**, 1-7.

HENRY, F.M. Physical education: An academic discipline. *Journal of Health, Physical Education and Recreation*, 1964, **35**, 32-33; 69.

HENRY, F.M. The academic discipline of physical education. *Quest*, 1978, **29**, 13-29.

LARSON, L.S. Professional preparation for the activity sciences. *Journal of Sports Medicine*, 1965, **5**, 15-22.

LAWSON, H.A., & Morford, W.R. The crossdisciplinary nature of kinesiology and sports studies: Distinctions, implications, and advantages. *Quest*, 1979, **31**(2), 222-230.

SHEEHAN, T. Sport: The focal point of physical education. *Quest*, 1968, **10**, 59-67.

SIEDENTOP, D. *Physical education: Introductory analysis*. Dubuque, IA: W.C. Brown, 1980.

CHAPTER 4
The art and science of performance

In the last chapter, we observed that the disciplinary movement created change and controversy in physical education and spawned a question that remains important today: What is the body of knowledge for the profession? Although debate is still heard over the disciplinary part of this body of knowledge, another part is less debatable—human performance in play, games, contests, dance, exercise, and sport. As an accepted part of the profession's subject matter, it will now be considered.

Human performance in these activities clearly has always been a part of the field's body of knowledge, whether in higher, secondary or elementary education. Moreover, performance appears as a central theme in virtually every definition for physical education. Indeed, this book began by asserting that physical education by any name is still a performance-based field.

Both disciplinary frameworks also grant an important place to performance. The pedagogical framework is designed to gain understanding that will facilitate human learning and performance; its aim is to provide guidelines for teachers and coaches who work with performers. The other framework, proclaimed by Henry and others, has as its objective the understanding of human performance in sport, dance, exercise, and the like. It assumes that the experience of performing provides only partial clues for this understanding, and that as a consequence a serious scholarly and scientific study of performance is essential. Therefore, both frameworks acknowledge that performance has an important role, suggesting that actual human experience in activity forms will remain as important to the profession's future as it has to its past.

This is not to imply that we lack questions and concerns about performance in physical education, however. Ironically enough, the more we learn about performance, the more related questions arise in connection with it. Of particular interest is the relationship between the nature of play, sport, and the like, the reasons why people are attracted to these activities, the consequences of their performances in them, and the ways in which these consequences may be useful or problematic. And the questions only begin here.

What is the future role of physical education in relation to human involvement in these activities? What outcomes are expected from any such involvement? When is it best to introduce this instruction? What role does performance play in an undergraduate degree program for physical education? Was Conant correct in recommending that all such courses be eliminated and that incoming undergraduates should demonstrate proficiency upon entering the major? If such classes are to be retained in higher education, should they emphasize methods and materials for teaching the activity, or skillful performance, or both?

As you can see, a host of questions surround this part of physical education that we take for granted. A few such questions are selected for the discussion ahead, with an aim to introduce the topic of human performance, not exhaust it. In fact, any attempt to exhaust the topic would raise more questions than it answered.

The Definitional Problem

Activity for physical education has been defined with terms such as play, games, dance, sport, exercise, and physical activity. The field's literature reveals yet other descriptors such as movement activities, motor performance, sport skills, and movement forms. In addition, classes in physical education for performance often are labeled "activity courses" as if everyone knew the only important kind of activity is that involving the human body. These and other examples raise an important question: Are these just word games, or do they indicate a problem in the profession?

For an answer, look at the functions of words. Words are powerful symbols for communication, vital in a profession that requires precision in the ways professionals speak about their work. Moreover, words indicate personal meaning; when people use different terminology there is little reason to believe they have a common understanding. That is, their uses of different words leads to the conclusion that they are not talking about, or even thinking about, the same things. Therefore, this first section of the chapter is devoted to the identification and discussion of a few terms so that we can enjoy a common understanding.

A common terminology for the profession results over time from the reasoned choices its members make among alternative ways to describe the same thing(s). Some ways of describing human performance and performance classes have already been identified. These descriptions might be called operational definitions because they represent how writers have chosen to talk about certain matters in a given context. Operational definitions are equally important in research. Thus, whether they are used in formal scholarship or in informal communication among peers, operational definitions can save time and help avoid confusion. The first goal, then, is to form an operational definition for activities that invite human physical performance.

Chapter 2 established that even though physical education differs from play, games, sport, and exercise, physical educators nevertheless have used these activities to achieve their objectives. Furthermore, these activities are part of the subject matter for the field. In order to avoid repeating *ad infinitum* the terms play, games, dance, and sport, we need to identify a descriptor for them. These forms of play can be called *ludic* activities. (The adjective "ludic" stems from the Latin word *ludus*, which originally meant a game.) Such a description is appropriate for these activities because, after all, they are forms of play. Furthermore, they form part of a larger class of ludic activities that includes playing a musical instrument and creating works of art. And the term "ludic" allows us to describe behavior in these activities by calling it *ludic behavior*, a term already appearing in the literature of our profession and its related fields.

Ludic activities as forms of play share some of play's essential features: Participation is voluntary; it is often removed from the demands and stresses of survival; its rewards are intrinsic, and so on. Yet, another class of activities has fallen into the realm of physical education. If play were at one end of a continuum, then this second group of activities would belong at the other end because they are more like modern conceptions of work. Participating in them is often described as a "workout." Examples include exercise regimens in the military, body-building activities, and compulsory calisthenics in a physical education class or a factory. Most appropriately called *physical activities*, these also form part of the subject matter for physical education.

In their efforts to define these activities, informed professionals must decide which are physical and which are ludic. Naturally, a gray area exists between the two kinds of activities and few of them are purely ludic *or* physical. For example, an industrial firm may use sport to improve employee work performance; here, sport stems from play but the sponsorship and conditions surrounding it are alien to play. On the other hand, an individual may participate regularly outside the school in a regimen of self-designed exercises. From start to finish, all the conditions of play may be in operation. Both cases require a value judgment based on operational definitions to determine whether an activity is primarily physical or ludic. It follows that one often must consider these activities as parts of the same whole. Though the two have been separated for ease of analysis here, frequently they are best discussed together using the conjunction "and." Therefore, physical and ludic activities comprise the performance base of the subject matter for physical education.

The Nature of Physical and Ludic Activities

An increasing number of scholars in many fields have directed their attention to physical and ludic activities, studying the different forms they take and how these forms and performance environments affect behavior. These studies have used animal and human subjects and employed many investigative methods. Such collective research has provided a better understanding of these activities, the behavior associated with them, and the parent society. A few examples will serve as an introduction to this area of study.

To begin with, humans throughout history have been attracted to physical and ludic activities. The growing body of knowledge gained through historical and cross-cultural analyses reveals a variety of ways in which people of different times and cultures have created and performed these activities. Thus we know that involvement has been extensive, but we are not sure why. One wonders how much was attributable to heredity and how much was triggered by the environment. But the fact remains that physical and ludic activities are being granted new importance. People are not just "recreated" by their participation in these forms; they also *create* physical and ludic activities that shape their culture (Huizinga, 1955).

A second consideration involves the motives for this participation and the meanings it imparts. Meanings and motives have varied among people throughout history, and many contemporary researchers in physical education have monitored them in our modern society. Not only have they identified an infinite variety of motives and meanings, but the historical literature indicates that those of today may change over time. Clearly, the task of studying · meanings and motives never ends.

The third consideration is related to the second. Human involvement in physical and ludic activities is characterized by a relationship between the activity selected, the environment in which it is performed, the special skills and equipment needed, and the performer's intent. Table 1 presents a continuum that may help you to analyze and classify human involvement in these activities and to appreciate how complex many are.

For example, the performer's motive(s) can range from instrumental (e.g., improving physical fitness, winning an athletic scholarship) to expressive (e.g., communicating a feeling or idea in dance, showing a hidden side of one's personality). The environment can range from the familiar confines of the local gymnasium to the potentially dangerous environment deep beneath the ocean's surface; indeed, the difference between the familiar or potentially dangerous performance environment serves as a distinction between high-risk and low-risk activities (Sparks, Note 1). And the activities themselves may range from highly structured and controlled to minimally structured—with control in the hands of the participant. These activities may also require high levels of skill and perhaps special equipment, or they may require minimal amounts of both. Fulfilling such requirements may depend on the participant's motives, as well as the extent to which the activity is structured or controlled by others and performed in a potentially

Table 1
Examples of Ways to Examine Physical and Ludic Activities

Performer's motives	Instrumental	Expressive
Amount of control by performer	Controlled by others	Controlled by performer
Characteristics of the activity	Highly structured	Largely unstructured
Prerequisites for performance	Requires special skills, knowledge, facilities, and equipment	No special requirements
Performance environment	Potentially hostile	Always friendly

dangerous environment. Involvement in activity clearly is a complex issue. An examination of the relationship between participant, activity, environment, and skills and equipment lends perspectives that enable us to better understand performance.

A fourth point is that researchers see an art, as well as a science, in performance. When a high level of performance skill is sought (e.g., for international and professional sport), understanding how best to elicit such performance from an athlete is invaluable in scientific study. Recent years have seen enormous growth in the number of scientists studying human physical performance (some of whom are among the new disciplinarians in physical education). Indeed, the quest for scientific information about performance has captured the attention of researchers worldwide.

The sport development systems in the Soviet Union and in the German Democratic Republic demonstrate that science can be built into coaching, teaching, and athletic training. These organizations even require that athletes, besides possessing superior performance skills, must understand the scientific principles affecting their performance. In addition to the sport scientists in Eastern Europe, an active group of scientists in North

America has also made extensive contributions to sport development. Their work has been equally valuable in the design of training and conditioning programs for amateur joggers.

This, then, serves as a basis for talking about the *science of performance*. In fact, two writers have suggested that scientific measurement endangers certain kinds of physical and ludic activities (Harper, 1973; Ingham, 1976); another has even suggested that sport in particular has become "a prisoner of measured time" (Brohm, 1978).

These authors are concerned that the expressive, or artistic, side of physical and ludic activities may be sacrificed if scientists continue their invasion. Their argument for an artistic side is easier to appreciate when forms of dance or some children's games are singled out for attention. Yet even highly structured sport allows artistic expression by individual players, expression that is considered art by some analysts. North Americans are not accustomed to calling physical and ludic activities art forms because their society assesses performance in quantifiable measures. The common concern is for won-loss records and a host of other statistics about individual and team performance. However, a more careful comparison of sport with other, more widely accepted art forms reveals that sport shares with them all the essential ingredients. Maheu's (1962) classic and insightful analysis yielded this finding along with the historical, sociological, and aesthetic features that prevent most people from seeing sport as an art form.

It is perhaps understandable that some do not see sport activities as forms of art, with performance as artistic expression, because they have not learned to think this way. But as professionals in physical education, we must gain such an understanding. After all, it will be our responsibility to cultivate in citizens the same understanding we've gained—that performance is both an *art* and a science.

A fifth finding is that performance in physical and ludic activities serves a variety of functions for the individual and society. Although debates continue on the matter, scholars have identified the important roles these activities play in child development. Others have found that these activities contributed to social cohesiveness through integration of diverse peoples and reinforcement of social order. In his classic work, *Homo Ludens* (1955), Huizinga suggests that culture is created as humans invent and participate in physical and ludic activities. But some scholars criticize such participation because they feel that it deflects people's attention from economic and social injustices that require reform and perhaps even revolution. These examples illustrate the relationship between human involvement in physical and ludic activities and the parent society.

The sixth finding is related to the fifth in that it addresses the consequences of this involvement for participants. Physical educators and others have believed that participation in these activities produces benefits such as improved physical fitness, good character, worthy use of leisure time, and a well-rounded personality. In fact, such presumed benefits are cited as objectives for many physical education programs today. But the question remains: Does research in this area document these claims? Do participants in physical and ludic activities actually gain such benefits by virtue of their participation? Evidence so far has not been conclusive, but some remain committed to these objectives.

This raises the proverbial question, "Which came first, the chicken or the egg?" Are people who share certain characteristics attracted to physical and ludic activities, or does participation in the activities produce those characteristics? This question continues to plague researchers, and until it is answered, many long-standing beliefs will need further review. Moreover, researchers point to some negative outcomes from excessive participation in these activities. Here, too, one must be cautious in assuming that personal beliefs provide a solid foundation for professional actions. After all, professionals are supposed to serve society on the basis of what they know and what they do.

For their part, some nonprofessionals have used physical and ludic activities for personal gain. Examples of this exist in other times and cultures as well as in our own history. The first intercollegiate athletic contest alluded to earlier may have been between crews from Harvard and Yale, for example, but it was sponsored by a railroad company interested in publicizing its new service. In addition, Berryman (1975) has documented how business firms have been using youth sport teams to advertise their products since the 1930s. These examples of the ways others have used physical and ludic activities to achieve personal, often commercial, objectives are at odds with professional ethics in physical education when participants are exploited in the name of profit.

For a professional group, this practice raises two other important issues, both stemming from understanding the nature of human involvement in physical and ludic activities. The first is whether physical educators in schools use these activities to achieve ends that are desirable and compatible with the activities themselves. The second issue is to what extent do the practices outside the schools serve all of society. In this light, physical educators may choose to adopt a cause going beyond their traditional mission. Having always been instrumental in encouraging more participation in these activities, physical educators may now find it necessary to protect participants and activities. That is, keeping commercialism away from ludic activities may be a worthy goal. It would provide a service to society, especially to its children. In this way, new knowledge could result in a new mission for our profession. For now, however, let's continue our study of the art and science of performance.

Education or Training in Physical and Ludic Activities?

Our introduction of the art and science of performance would be incomplete unless it examined the role of physical and ludic activities in education. To this end, consider your own experiences in performance classes. Think about these experiences as we proceed. Do they result in training, education, or both?

We should compare some of what we know with what we commonly try to do in these activity courses in higher education, beginning with some findings. Both animals and humans can be trained to perform physical and ludic activities. A trip to Sea World or to the local zoo reveals that seals can be trained to shoot baskets with remarkable accuracy; bears can learn to dance; gorillas can learn to perform gymnastic feats. Likewise, dogs and horses can be trained to run around race tracks and rats can learn to run treadmills. Obviously, performance is not restricted to physical education majors, or even to humans.

Human *training* in an activity has two characteristics. First, training usually is activity- or context-specific, so that skills learned in one situation will not necessarily transfer to others. Only when there is substantial similarity in the skills required for two activities will those from one transfer to the other. And, despite popular usage of the concept by sport broadcasters, a general "athletic ability" does not exist. Special or specific skills require equally specific training for their development.

Second, the training process normally does not emphasize self-directed learning. Training tends to result from and produce a dependence on the trainer or instructor. Of course, a person trained in an activity can continue to learn by trial and error techniques, but if a major change occurs in the activity or if systematic revisions are in order, the individual must be retrained. Speaking strictly of trained capacities, then, such a person can be compared *in principle* to a robot. Both must be reprogrammed as needed because self-directed change for them is the exception, not the rule. Put differently, people develop a trained incapacity to proceed on their own.

A trained person, therefore, is not the same as an educated person. An educated person certainly requires training in basic skills because these are part of the foundation for an education. (Indeed, such skills were identified as part of a liberal education in chapter 1.) But an educated person progresses *beyond* skilled performance to those qualities associated with being uniquely human. An educated person not only knows how to perform skillfully, but also knows the significance of such skills. Education, in other words, is much more than animal training. Unlike training that results in dependence, it produces an independent person and includes modes of expression, feeling, and understanding. Education is not context- or activity-specific. Rather, it presents skills in a general, possibly a theoretical, framework. An educated person is thus in a position to gauge the significance of self-selected and other-directed experiences and to change as necessary.

The distinction between education and training in and through physical and ludic activities can be approached another way: by identifying two different ways of knowing, or two different kinds of knowledge. Kretchmar (Note 2) explained this as knowing "how to" perform these activities versus knowing "about" them. Possession of one type of knowledge does not guarantee possession of the other. Countless athletes know how to perform but are unable to analyze scientifically their own performance. And no doubt some scientists can analyze performance but do not have the ability to actually perform. In these terms, the trained person knows "how to" but not "about," whereas the educated person must possess *both* kinds of knowledge. Educated persons can perform as well as analyze performance; they have received a *physical education*.

Having laid a foundation, let's return to some questions about physical and ludic activities in education. Do students who complete physical education classes in schools, colleges, and universities receive a physical training or a physical education? Do undergraduate physical education majors who complete performance classes receive an education or training? These are the kinds of questions that, as professionals in the field, we are encouraged to ask because we call ourselves physical *educators*. These questions are useful in checking how much our actions match our original intentions.

Performance Courses in the Undergraduate Major

What, then, can be said about activity courses in the major, considering that much of it is composed of such courses? Since performance in physical and ludic activities constitutes part of the subject matter for physical education, requirements for performance courses are not at all surprising. On the other hand, some important questions are surfacing in professional circles about these courses; they will be reviewed briefly.

James Bryant Conant raised the first issue in 1963; now increasing numbers of physical educators also are evaluating the responsibilities that secondary school physical education teachers have in preparing students for a career in physical education. The question really is, how much proficiency should incoming students in physical education be expected to demonstrate? Should they be proficient in one or many activities? And how can we evaluate such proficiency reliably and validly? These questions, significant today, promise to become even more so in the future. After all, the amount of knowledge and skill to be mastered in physical education keeps increasing and not all of it can be postponed until graduate education. Some material must be introduced earlier in the schools to facilitate the students' mastery over it.

Indeed, this is exactly what is happening in other subjects. High school students in chemistry, physics, and mathematics now confront subject matter formerly restricted to second-year students in college. By introducing this subject matter earlier, college and university programs can become more advanced. The result is a more highly educated student, one who knows nearly as much as the person earning a master's degree some 10 years earlier. This same result is possible in physical education. Steps already are underway to bring this about, such as expecting higher levels of performance competence upon entry, based on the role of high school teachers in professional education.

The question of how to evaluate such proficiency has accompanied the change and controversy of the disciplinary movement. Following the lead of Henry and his colleagues, some undergraduate programs award degrees for work roles other than teaching; yet performance courses remain an important part of the education. Other programs, following the lead of those who see pedagogy as the appropriate disciplinary framework, include separate courses complete with laboratories for developing teacher skills. Thus, the question in both circumstances is the extent to which performance courses should contain methods and materials for teaching the activity. Is the purpose of the course to develop performance skill in volleyball, to learn how to teach volleyball, or both? Naturally this question applies to all performance classes, not just volleyball. How it has been answered by physical educators serves to differentiate one kind of undergraduate program from the others. This question will continue to demand attention from persons in the profession because it is related to another issue.

Why can't students specialize in just a few activities, rather than having to gain exposure to many? Furthermore, why is it not possible for students to earn a degree centered on their performance in a single activity, or a related cluster of activities? Such a degree is already possible in dance at many university campuses. Why not expand the opportunity to include other forms of physical and ludic activity? After all, physical education is a performance-based field, just like music, art, and drama. In those fields, students may graduate with specialization in a few activities or instruments. Many students seek such a degree because they plan to perform for a number of years following graduation. Why not offer the same opportunity in physical education? This kind of question is fun. It prompts professionals to examine the assumptions supporting existing operations and signals prospective directions for the future. These important outcomes, then, stem from reflections about the uses of physical and ludic activities in physical education.

Summary

The evolution of modern physical education has been linked to human involvement in physical and ludic activities, which are appropriately considered part of the subject matter for physical education, a performance-based field. Many deep concerns have arisen about performance, its increasing popularity, and research into its dynamics. An understanding of them is essential for effective practice.

Interestingly, operational definitions are needed in discussing the activities that form part of physical education. As the field develops its own terminology, those definitions will ultimately be chosen among a number of alternative definitions for the same thing(s). The mere presence of such an advanced terminology will point to the field's maturation. For present purposes, however, physical and ludic activities comprise part of physical education's subject matter, and the correlates and consequences of ludic behavior are of interest to all members in the profession.

The research on physical and ludic activities has increased over the past decade, accompanied by new findings about human involvement in them. These findings demonstrate that humans have a long history of involvement in physical and ludic activities, they harbor a variety of meanings and motives concerning these activities, their involvement can be analyzed through certain perspectives, and some individuals and groups use these activities for personal or commercial gain. In this last connection it may be as important for physical educators to consider *protecting* these activities, and the human involvement therein, as it has been to encourage such involvement in the first place.

As for the role of physical and ludic activities in physical education, several important issues surface, the first of which pertains to the outcomes of such activities. Are the outcomes consistent with a physical training or a physical education? Although training is indeed part of a good education, an education transcends mere training because it enables one to understand the activity in addition to knowing how to perform it. Education results in independence, not dependence, and the educated person knows the meaning and significance of what has been mastered.

Other questions pertain to the role of physical and ludic activities in the undergraduate major. One centers on the extent to which methods and materials for teaching activities should be included in courses. Another is directed toward the responsibilities that high school teachers have in the professional preparation of their students, and implies that performance competency should be developed before the students enter undergraduate education.

The third question raises the possibility of greater specialization in performance, even to the point where an entire undergraduate degree could be structured around a single activity or a related group of activities.

Because performance in physical and ludic activities is the basis for so many of the operations in physical education, future professionals must learn how to perform these activities and must gain a wealth of information about them. For in addition to wearing a real whistle, teachers, coaches and other professionals must be prepared to blow a symbolic whistle to stop practices that depart from professional standards.

Supplementary Activities

Self-testing Exercises

After reading chapter 4, you should be able to:

1. Explain why a common terminology is needed in physical education;
2. Identify physical and ludic activities in describing the range and wealth of performance included in physical education;
3. Identify exemplary areas of research into human involvement in physical and ludic activities and cite some of the findings;
4. Discuss potential roles of professionals in physical education in dealing with physical and ludic activities;
5. Identify important questions about the extent to which performance is a basis for education or training;
6. Apply knowledge about training and education to important questions surrounding the role of performance in undergraduate physical education.

Class Activities

1. Interview participants in physical and ludic activities to learn their reasons for participation. Be certain to include people of all ages and skill levels, from a wide variety of activities. As a class, develop a profile of involvements in physical and ludic activities stemming from the findings of the class.
2. Interview faculty members to get their views on the role(s) of

performance classes in physical education. Determine how the views of faculty members vary as a function of their own interests.

Questions for Discussion

1. Should teaching methods be included in performance courses? If so, what are the advantages and disadvantages?
2. Should it be possible to complete an undergraduate major in physical education and kinesiology without completing any performance courses? Why, or why not?
3. What is the relationship between performance skill and public school teaching in physical education? Must a person possess skill in an activity in order to teach it?
4. What is the relationship between physical education and kinesiology?
5. In your view, what are the objectives for performance courses in your own college or university? Are these courses restricted to undergraduate majors in physical education and kinesiology? Should they be? Should these performance courses be modified? If so, how?
6. Can performance skill be included in a definition of a liberal education? Explain.

Sources for Additional Reading

CALLOIS, R. *Man, play, and games.* New York: The Free Press of Glencoe, 1961.

HUIZINGA, J. *Homo Ludens: A study of the play-element in culture.* Boston: Beacon Press, 1955.

KRETCHMAR, R.S. In search of structure: Perspectives of the discipline. *NAPEHE Annual Conference Proceedings, 1979,* Vol. I.

LAWSON, H.A., & Pugh, D.L. Six significant questions about performance and performance courses in the major. *Journal of Physical Education, Recreation, and Dance,* 1981, 52(3), 59-61.

CHAPTER 5
The missions and subject matter of physical education

Physical education is a rapidly changing profession, and change has sparked controversy. Even the profession's leaders find it difficult to agree on all the relevant issues. Today's challenge is to strive for a new basis for compromise, one that allows more consensus. This requires designing a framework to accommodate the interests of the majority in the profession.

Now is the time to meet this challenge. Indeed, the challenge of the 1980s is like the one confronting the profession's founders almost 100 years ago: to mesh competing approaches into one framework called physical education. Luther Halsey Gulick, an early leader in the profession, accepted the challenge by providing a framework that included gymnastics, exercises for preventive medicine, and sports and games. His work was a model of cooperation in a field split by competition and controversy. Yet Gulick had only proposed a framework. The unity he envisioned resulted because others in the profession were equally committed to compromise and consensus. No less is our challenge in the 1980s. We can propose frameworks of all kinds, but there is little hope of realizing them unless the profession's members are committed to finding common ground.

Some members in the profession have "pet" interests and views, which is both natural and appropriate. After all, groups or segments within the profession grow as people with similar interests and views come together. In this sense, life in a profession is full of debate among competing groups, as was the case when Gulick faced the profession 100 years ago; it still is now. These competing groups are a sign of the profession's good health because they inject an internal stimulus for change and their presence suggests that members care very much about the future of the field. Thus, this kind of conflict is good, *if* it is managed properly and *if* an appropriate framework for more debate and compromise can be employed.

At the root of proper conflict management and debate are the skills of effective communication. Not only must people express their views clearly and concisely, but more importantly, they must be good listeners. In order to be a good listener, you must temporarily suspend personal ideas and try to put yourself in the place of your adversary. While this is always difficult to do, it is the surest way to free communication, a communication that is indispensable in a profession. So suspend for a time your own ideas and be a good listener as the following discussion unfolds. Then take an active role in expressing *your* views on these related issues. Remember, *all* such views are important as we try to reach new compromises and a greater degree of consensus.

The Missions of Physical Education

Any framework designed to unite rather than divide the profession must somehow accommodate the advocates of the two disciplinary concepts (Henry's and the pedagogical counterpart) as well as those interested in performance skills. In so doing, the subject matter offered from each of the three perspectives must merge into a workable whole. Although the task could begin with a discussion of the field's subject matter, a better approach is to initiate discussion through an analysis of the field's missions.

The history of modern physical education is clearly linked to the schools, and education more generally. Latter-day colleagues have devoted their attention to the important mission of starting and then improving secondary and elementary school programs, as well as those in higher education. Their efforts were quite successful and were founded upon the belief that these programs met the needs of students and, in turn, society. They also believed that when these needs were not met the consequences would be serious for both individuals and society. What, then, were these needs?

Our colleagues wanted to develop and maintain physical fitness in students who needed it. They wanted to develop sport skills in students who needed to learn how to use leisure time appropriately, and they wanted to foster in students desirable traits such as loyalty and citizenship. They believed that a sports and games curriculum, offered as part of life adjustment education, would give people these skills, beliefs, and values that would last a lifetime. To be sure, our colleagues encountered disappointments, but they were confident that improvements in the preparation of teachers and coaches would do much to rectify the situation. They also had faith that their research would improve the methods they employed to achieve their mission. These are among the legacies of the most recent past, and many will remain so in the near future. But is there not more to the future missions of physical education?

This question can be answered by raising other questions and by granting that physical education programs remain a central mission in this scenario. The importance of physical education programs, together with needed improvements for teacher education and research, must be assessed against a larger question. Should physical education in the future be limited to schools?

Let's look at this issue through the lens of history. Physical and ludic activities at one time were largely restricted to schools and urban playgrounds. Today, however, the increase in opportunities and places for participation brings with it an accompanying increase in possibilities for professional employment in community recreation centers, private and public sports clubs, dance companies, and day care centers. In a few places, such employment opportunities are almost as plentiful as those for teaching and coaching in schools. Should physical educators seek both kinds of jobs? Should we offer appropriate education and training for them? Are people who fill these jobs members of the profession of physical education? To answer these questions, one must look beyond the present as conditioned by the past and think about the future in a new light.

The most basic question goes right to the heart of the profession. One must ask whether members of the profession can continue believing that the school and its programs such as physical education will prepare people for a lifetime. There is room for doubt here. For example, studies on how adults spend their leisure time suggest that what people do is a function of their situation. It makes a difference if one is married or single, male or female, young or old, upper-middle class or lower class, and living in a rural or urban area. Furthermore, some of these circumstances change frequently; people are more mobile than ever before, divorce rates are high, and career changes are common. Because it is nearly impossible to anticipate all the changes that will occur in individuals and in society, it is risky to assume that we can give adolescents in school everything they will need for a lifetime. The school and its physical education programs are important in forming lifetime skills and attitudes, but doubts are increasing as to whether this is the only way.

For these and other reasons, many in the profession have already expanded their definition of physical education by increasing its range of missions. Not content to rely upon the school and its programs alone, these colleagues have tried to reach people other than students in agencies outside the school. They first placed prospective teachers in these agencies but later decided that teacher education is not altogether appropriate for some kinds of employment. Consequently, they have accepted the responsibility for designing and implementing degree programs in physical education for careers other than teaching, such as exercise counseling, sport management, sport journalism, and cardiac rehabilitation. Proponents of these programs consider them as part of the new missions for physical education, and the graduates of these programs as members of the profession of physical education.

This surely expands the view of the profession's missions and membership, but it does not lessen the importance of school programs, teachers, and coaches. Rather, this expanded view begins with attention to school-age children and continues with attention to people after they leave school. In short, these missions touch people's needs, problems, and aspirations throughout life.

If this view of the profession's missions becomes widely accepted, along with its expanded definition of the profession's membership, then important implications can be derived for the field's subject matter and its degree programs in higher education. In fact, indications are that this view is gaining greater acceptance among the profession's members because conditions are ripe for such a change. For example, there are fewer opportunities to teach in schools. And, to return to a point made in chapter 3, colleges and universities still must demonstrate their uniqueness in comparison to others; new degree programs for careers other than teaching attest to their success in this. Perhaps most important is that students now choose to major in physical education because they already know that they can be prepared for careers other than teaching. Physical education may have to become something more because these students and other people will not allow it to be anything less.

A Framework for the Field's Subject Matter

A direct relationship exists between questions of mission and questions of subject matter; having addressed the former, we now turn to subject matter. In building a framework for the subject matter of physical education, one must avoid either-or thinking. It is not a question of Henry's disciplinary framework *or* that for pedagogy, nor is it a case of performance skills *or* disciplinary knowledge. These all form parts of physical education's subject matter because each promises to improve the work of the profession. Consequently, the challenge in building a new framework is to identify the contributions of each and, even more importantly, to pinpoint the relationships among these parts.

The next step is to define this subject matter. The subject matter of physical education consists of the art and science of human involvement in physical and ludic activities, together with the knowledge, sensitivities, and skills employed by professionals who work with these activities. We can amplify this definition and identify the relationships between the parts of this subject matter in the following discussion.

The Art and Science of Performance

One can come to understand the art and science of performance in two related ways. First, this is achieved by direct exposure to physical and ludic activities, whether in formal physical education classes or elsewhere. The training inherent in this exposure results in improved skills and invaluable rewards. There is no adequate substitute for this direct experience with activity; in fact, any claims we make for knowing activities such as tennis and golf must be documented by our experience with them.

One can come to understand performance in a second way—through prolonged, serious study of it. There is no shortage of information here, thanks to the ever increasing research in the profession. Scientists and scholars have used physiological, psychological, biomechanical, sociological, historical, philosophical, and neurological perspectives to gain new knowledge. Disciplinary knowledge, in Henry's sense of the terms, has revealed a tremendous amount of insight into performance. This body of knowledge may be defined as

> the socio-historical and contemporary roles of physical and ludic activities in culture, in both primitive and advanced societies, and the contribution of these activities to the emotional, social, physical, and aesthetic development of the individual; and,

> selected biological, psychological, and mechanical factors which are associated with the individual's growth and motor development, functional status, and abilities to engage in physical and ludic activities. (Morford, Lawson, & Hutton, 1981)

This body of knowledge and the performance skills gained through direct experience are equally important to a complete understanding of performance, and they may enjoy a special relationship that pays dividends for professionals.

Performance experiences and performance analysis are really opposite sides of the same coin; and just as a coin is not a coin without both sides, so too does physical education require both parts of this subject matter for its identity. Surely personal experiences lend greater meaning to scientific and scholarly analysis. Because we have played basketball, analysis of it tells us as much about ourselves as it does about basketball. In the same vein, knowledge gained through scientific and scholarly study can be used to improve performance skills and experiences. Like many elite athletes in Eastern Europe, through such study we gain the ability to criticize intelligently our own performances as well as others', and this ability becomes part of an education. Thus, experiences in the classroom, laboratory, gymnasium, and playing fields are complementary. That these two sides of the field's subject matter may be blended together so easily is one of their most important and attractive features.

However, this special relationship gets lost in definitions for the disciplinary knowledge for physical education such as Henry's; this is unfortunate because it becomes difficult for people to compromise. You may recall that Henry in 1964 insisted that all disciplinary knowledge existed apart from real world application, and many agreed with him. Yet it is apparent from the preceding discussion that a great deal of knowledge gained by studying human performance is immediately useful. The question, then, may be less one of the applicability of this knowledge and more one of what it will not accomplish for professionals. It will not provide workers in the profession with all the knowledge, skills, and sensitivities that they will require in their work. This takes professional knowledge, which is related to disciplinary knowledge in some ways but different from it in others. Let's now turn to this professional knowledge, acknowledging that disciplinary knowledge in the tradition of Henry has more immediate applications to the real world than was first claimed.

Professional Knowledge

A discipline for physical education serves to enlighten members of the profession about important questions concerning practice. As professionals solve the mysteries of human involvement in physical and ludic activities, they will be able to perform their work in a more intelligent way. Such is the promise of disciplinary knowledge, which, though insufficient by itself, becomes foundational when added to performance experiences.

A professional possesses such a foundation *and* the knowledge, sensitivities, and skills to apply it. To return to the second disciplinary framework presented in chapter 3, this is the kind of outcome that advocates of pedagogy had in mind for teachers. Yet the same needs arise with careers other than teaching. In this view, there is no reason to separate theory from practice because professional knowledge, although theoretical, is eminently practical. Let's examine this point more closely.

This professional knowledge, like that gained about the art and science of performance, may be achieved in two ways: by direct experiences and by prolonged, serious study. Research is just as important in developing professional knowledge as it is in its disciplinary counterpart, and it is every bit as sophisticated. The results of this research are somewhat different in that they are immediately useful to practitioners, which is surely an advantage as well as a distinctive feature. But professional knowledge is related to knowledge about the art and science of human performance, as illustrated in the three following examples.

First, teachers in school physical education programs usually are charged with the task of improving their students' physical fitness. Which activities should they choose? How should they design and conduct exercise programs for students? Understanding the art and science of performance helps to answer these questions, but actual teaching is not so easy. What incentives might you offer to students who achieve their goals? What teaching techniques will facilitate students' learning and performance? These questions suggest the need for professional knowledge. In order for the school physical education teacher to be effective, he or she must have a command of professional knowledge that is wedded to the foundational knowledge about the art and science of performance.

As a second example, coaches for team sports always face the problem of trying to increase team cohesiveness so that they can enhance the social interaction among players and improve team performance. A good coach would read the research available on team cohesiveness and group dynamics in sport, incorporating this information into the planning for practices. Here again, though, differences exist between thinking about (or planning) and actually performing the work. To be successful, a good coach must understand coaching behavior and be able to act accordingly. In other words, good coaches are not prepared just to think about their work; they must also do it. Their ability to do it stems from their professional knowledge.

Sport programmers who work in community recreation centers are a third example. Often they must design opportunities for a wide range of people possessing an equally wide range of motives and interests. Some people wish to be educated, others wish to play, and still others wish to achieve new heights in their performance. Is it possible to accommodate them all? How? The programmer would begin by drawing upon knowledge about human involvement in physical and ludic activities, directing attention toward factors that either facilitate or interfere with participation. In addition, he or she would consider whether educational, recreational, and elite models for sport should exist side by side in the same agency.

All this is part of the planning phase, and the work only begins here. A host of questions remain about the implementation, administration, and evaluation of the programs. Only through a professional body of knowledge can the programmer answer these questions and perform his or her role because both kinds of knowledge are necessary for job performance.

It is clear, then, that professional knowledge has an important relationship to the art and science of performance. The same relationship between foundational, disciplinary knowledge and professional knowledge can be found in other professions. For example, if professional knowledge were not important, medical doctors would need only complete coursework in physiology and chemistry; social workers only in sociology; lawyers only in philosophy and history. The same is true for physical education. Professional knowledge is indispensable for effective performance in our work.

On the other hand, we must emphasize that all professional knowledge requires an appropriate foundation. It is difficult to imagine doctors who do not know physiology and chemistry, social workers who have not mastered sociology, and lawyers who have not studied philosophy and history. It is equally difficult to imagine how physical educators could be effective if they had not mastered foundational knowledge about the art and science of performance in physical and ludic acivities. An important feature of this knowledge is that it is gained by actually performing these activities, not just by studying them. Personal performance skills are just as important as their analytical counterparts in connection with foundational and professional knowledge.

The point is that the subject matter for the profession of physical education fits together to form a desirable and logical whole. The experience of performing, the analysis of performance, and the knowledge and skills for their application and use are strongly related. To be sure, professional knowledge for careers other than teaching and coaching awaits further development because these careers represent new missions for the profession. Yet this framework for thinking about the subject matter for physical education, and its relationship to the field's missions, actually highlights the importance of such knowledge in the future and suggests ways in which it can be easily accommodated.

All such frameworks mark but a beginning, not a destination. They offer clues, not answers. This does not suggest that every college and university must offer career preparation for every conceivable job, nor does it imply the existence of one, best system for organizing the profession's subject matter into courses of study. Nor does it suggest that such a framework should escape careful review, criticism, discussion, and revision by old and new members of the profession.

The fact remains, however, that visions for the profession's future can emerge from such a consideration of the field's missions, subject matter, and their relationship. It is not just a matter of what the field has been, but what it can become. The task is not so much one of forecasting the future as it is one of *creating* it. If we in the profession are to succeed in our efforts to create our future, then nothing short of a united front will be required. The discussion thus far has been directed at such a united front, but the real work lies ahead. Much of the work will rest in the hands of the new members in the profession—the introductory students of today. This invitation to physical education is extended to those who welcome the work and are excited about the challenges.

Summary

Physical education is a profession in transition. Change in the profession inevitably causes differences of opinion among its members about fundamental questions such as the proper mission(s) of the field, its subject matter, and the appropriate organization and conduct of physical education programs. The conflict and debate arising over these questions can be good for the profession if the interchanges are managed well. Handled properly, they may unite the profession; handled improperly, they may cause it to splinter.

A challenge confronting physical educators in the years ahead is one of resolving internal differences to a greater degree. The extent to which the profession can create a desirable future for itself, and for society, appears to hinge upon our ability to compromise in seeking consensus. A framework for compromise and consensus must accommodate competing positions and promise more services to society.

The field's mission in the past has been limited largely to school physical education programs and the preparation of teachers and coaches. While this will continue to be an important mission, new definitions of physical education will likely emerge in the future. Physical education, once restricted to schools and teachers, will come to mean work and workers in a variety of agencies, all centered around physical and ludic activities.

The subject matter of the field permits such a vision to materialize. Logical and desirable relationships exist between the art and science of performance and professional knowledge necessary for work. Coupled with the expanded missions for the field, this subject matter provides a framework for the profession's future, serving to guide and unite it. Yet all such frameworks mark only a beginning and should not hide the fact that the profession's members are the most important ingredient in its future.

Supplementary Activities

Self-testing Exercises

After reading chapter 5, you should be able to:

1. State your views on the mission(s) of physical education and be prepared to justify them;
2. Identify the subject matter of physical education and the relationships between the parts of this subject matter;
3. Discuss the importance of unity in the profession.

Class Activities

1. Debate the subject matter and role of physical education as a profession. Have class members read the important works of the field's leaders and play their parts during the debate. Then try to reach a compromise on the issues they have identified.
2. Interview school physical education teachers to get their views on the extent to which the school can accomplish all the goals that people have set for it.

Questions for Discussion

1. Is the concern over disciplines and their format justifiable? Important? Or just another example of academic games that people play?
2. Does it matter if prospective teachers of physical education study kinesiology? Why, or why not?
3. Does it matter if prospective teachers of physical education study pedagogy? Why, or why not?
4. Should all of the knowledge and skill you acquire in your undergraduate major apply directly and immediately to your chosen career? Why, or why not?
5. Should we establish separate departments of physical education and kinesiology? Why, or why not?
6. Are there other ways to join together in the same profession everyone who works with physical and ludic activities? What are they?

Sources for Additional Reading

LAWSON, H.A. Looking back from the year 2082. *Journal of Physical Education, Recreation and Dance*, 1982, **53**(4), 15-18.

LOCKE, L.F. From research in the discipline to practice in the profession: One more time. *Proceedings of the NCPEAM/ NAPECW Conference*, 1977, pp. 34-45.

SINGER, R.N. Future directions for the movement arts and sciences. *Quest*, 1979, **31**(2), 255-263.

CHAPTER 6
Careers and career planning in physical education

A new view of the missions and subject matter of physical education has been presented, one in which many careers were identified briefly. Now we must examine careers and career planning more closely, being mindful of the field's recent evolution. Until the mid-1970s fewer career choices were available in physical education. Before that, an undergraduate degree usually meant preparation for teaching and coaching.

Teaching and coaching remain viable, important options for physical education students, of course, but they no longer are the only options. In fact, so many opportunities exist for different kinds of work with physical and ludic activities that often it is difficult to decide which is the best choice. Consequently, we must devote our attention to the process of career planning as it affects this choice, as well as to the careers themselves.

Considerations in Planning

Planning any endeavor requires looking into the future and attempting to match expected circumstances and opportunities with personal goals. Naturally these goals are not limited to employment alone, but include a range of interests and involvements that together will comprise one's total lifestyle. Indeed, in the course of their career planning many people make the mistake of thinking only about employment instead of considering how that career will affect the way they live. For example, a number of persons leave teaching because of its low salaries or because the combined work of teaching and coaching consumes too much time and energy. Some of these conditions may change in the near future but other parts may not. This issue, at the heart of career planning, requires one to make thoughtful decisions about lifestyle in general, for only then is it possible to make a balanced assessment of career choices about salary, working conditions, and the time and energy required for work. These decisions are so important that they merit extensive fact-finding, discussions, and deliberations.

People change jobs today more than ever before, which is comforting in the sense that it implies today's decisions are not always binding. Yet the mere fact that so many do change their work should alert us to other considerations; for example, many of these people may not have given enough attention to career planning earlier in their lives. Or, perhaps they did include plans for such a career change. That is, some may have anticipated the likelihood of such change and thus undertaken a program of studies facilitating the transition from one kind of work to another. Liberal education, as defined in chapter 1, lays the foundation for such a change, but more specific courses and experiences may be needed to facilitate future transition. In this sense, additional coursework completed now is like a financial investment; the time and energy required today may pay valuable dividends tomorrow.

Other basic considerations in career planning are best highlighted by returning to this important distinction: There is a difference between having a job and pursuing a career. A career implies membership in a profession and includes a high level of commitment, together with the expectation, at least initially, that membership in the profession will last a lifetime. In this light, the following questions should probe deeper into your own values and aspirations.

How important is it for you to earn a large salary? How much salary will you need to pursue the lifestyle you have envisioned? What are you good at? To what extent are your skills, aptitudes, and interests included in the career you are considering? What are the criteria for success in that career? Does it contain opportunities for promotion and advancement? Do you stand a good chance of succeeding, being promoted, and gaining the fulfillment of personal accomplishment? Is this work performed by older people or restricted to the very young? If the latter is true, what should be included in your studies now to enable you to change careers when you get older? Do you prefer work that allows you to remain physically active? Is your preference today likely to be appropriate 20 years from now? How important is it for you to have complete control over your work? Do you like routines, or are you the kind of person who cannot tolerate a lot of repetition in the workplace? Does your chosen career require additional education and training? If so, how much and at what cost? Will your work serve society in some way? If so, is this important in its own right?

These are just a few questions you must consider in planning your career. There is no single, "right" answer. Instead, these questions lend a framework for important personal decisions about the future.

Exemplary Career Opportunities

A primary purpose of an introductory course in any field is to identify the subject matter and its potential uses, one of which paves the way to a career and another of which guides the career. This is a major characteristic of professional work; in physical education it implies an obligation to gain mastery over the field's subject matter and to use it in performing the work.

The range of career options is determined largely by the scope and kind of subject matter for a field. In this light, all competing definitions of the subject matter for physical education must be examined—including the framework already presented as well as other, more restricted definitions of the missions and subject matter of physical education. Here, too, a direct relationship exists between the subject matter you master and the kind of work it allows you to perform. However, a distinct advantage of the framework presented in the last chapter is that its expansiveness makes possible many career opportunities in physical education, including the option of teaching and coaching in schools.

If this framework is accepted in principle, then any professional role in the work world for physical and ludic activities can be developed as a degree program in higher education. Now re-read the previous sentence. Upon closer examination, it merits at least two qualifying statements.

The first concerns the notion of becoming a professional and pursuing a career. Any *professional* role, as opposed to job, can have a parent, university degree program. This is because some jobs do not entail the obligation to use theory and research in work, to offer services to others, or to otherwise signify professional work. An undergraduate degree is not required for these jobs, nor does the work itself require highly educated people. Community colleges, technical and vocational institutes, and hiring organizations themselves prepare people for many such jobs. In contrast to higher education, the training these agencies provide is less expensive, more efficient, and more appropriate. Certainly these jobs are important, but the issue here is not one of their fundamental worth. Instead we seek to distinguish what kinds of work can be targeted for a degree program in higher education, for in this sense colleges and universities provide a special kind of vocation—a profession.

A second qualification for the earlier statement stems from the rapid rate of change in physical education. Although people with degrees in physical education perform a variety of work roles, including teaching and coaching, the design and conduct of study programs for careers other than teaching are still experimental. Why? Consider two possibilities: Many kinds of careers have yet to be created, and formal degree programs do not exist for every conceivable career that one might choose to pursue in physical education. These possibilities imply that depending upon the career in question, a great deal of independent planning and preparation may be necessary. Some of the career opportunities in physical education are listed in Table 2. Although this list is not comprehensive, it does illustrate multiple uses for the subject matter of physical education, and it suggests the range of missions that professionals in the field have within their grasp. Table 2 also shows that *bona fide* choices regarding a career are available in principle to any student in physical education. The question remains, on what basis do you make a choice?

Career planning can also be approached by considering the kind of preparation necessary for the career and the nature of this work as it is currently performed. Each merits additional discussion.

Table 2
Career Opportunities in Physical Education and Kinesiology

Researcher in pedagogy or kinesiology
College or university faculty member
Sport manager
Sport planner and programmer
Movement, dance, or recreational therapist
Stress manager
School physical education teacher
Perceptual-motor specialist for early childhood education programs
Sport journalist
Sport broadcaster
Recreational director
Teaching professional for sports in private clubs and public agencies
Cardio-pulmonary rehabilitation specialist
Athletic trainer
Sport physician
Coach
Consultant for sport facilities or equipment
Specialist in physical fitness and exercise prescription
Salesperson for sporting goods industry
Industrial sports specialist
Leisure counselor
Physical therapist
Sport nutritionist
Professional athlete
Computer programmer for sport agencies
Resort or camp director
Sport psychologist
Fitness director
Youth sports director

Building Blocks in a Professional Degree Program

Many kinds of courses in physical education package different kinds of knowledge, sensitivities, and skills. As the building blocks for career preparation, these courses parallel the degree program in physical education. Some are courses for developing performance skills, some are disciplinary courses that analyze human involvement in physical and ludic activities, from a given perspective, and some are professional courses that apply knowledge and develop skill for a particular career.

The coursework sequence may vary somewhat, depending upon the degree program and the potential career. Yet prevailing patterns of career preparation can be identified; for example, in most institutions, coursework for liberal education lays the foundation (Stiles, 1974) and specific courses in physical education follow.

Courses in performance and performance analysis customarily build from and enhance the liberal education foundation (Morford & Lawson, 1978). The common requirements you will find in performance and performance analysis for all physical education majors comprise a core curriculum designed to help you master the breadth of the subject matter. It also gives future professionals a common knowledge base, acquaints them with the terminology and, above all, lends credence to the claim that all are members of the same profession regardless of the career selected.

In other words, breadth of study is prerequisite to depth of study and specialization for work roles. Once this fundamental principle is identified, the roles of other building blocks can be assigned readily. Additional coursework in selected areas of performance and performance analysis, with emphasis on the chosen career, should follow core requirements in the major. In addition, one should select professional-level courses within and outside of physical education that reflect career choice. Among these professional-level courses are those devoted to the dissemination of theory and research; however, field experiences are equally important in preparing for any career. In the following three examples (Morford & Lawson, 1978), performance courses and performance analysis courses—divided into sport studies and motor control—are first in sequence with the others coming later.

The first example should interest those who think they might like careers in sport planning, programming, and management. The concept of career preparation for these related roles is illustrated in Figure 2. The innermost circle at the base of the triangle represents performance courses and experiences; the outer circle, performance analysis or disciplinary courses. The relationship between the two is thus viewed as complementary where each informs the other.

One portion of the disciplinary coursework is highlighted by shading (Figure 2), suggesting that this area of study, called sport studies, is pursued in some depth. Why? Because knowledge about sport, including how it functions and operates in society, is indispensable for people wishing to plan, manage, and evaluate it in a professional manner. Accepting this premise can help in your career decisions, for clearly, a person interested in sport manage-

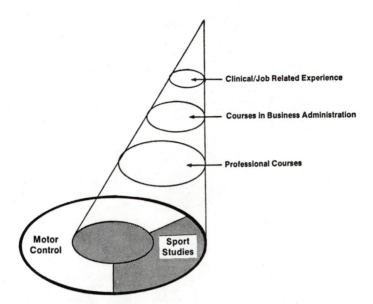

Figure 2. A degree program in sport management.

ment should also be interested in studying sport's operations in society from sociological, historical, anthropological, and philosophical perspectives. Interest and competence in the subject matter of the career are very important considerations in one's choice among alternatives.

Yet a closer inspection of Figure 2 reveals that a sociocultural study of sport alone is not sufficient to prepare people for careers in sport planning, programming, and management. They need other building blocks. Moving up the triangle, then, implies greater depth and specialization in the form of professional-level courses such as programming, administration, and evaluation, in addition to the all-important field experiences or internships. Figure 2 also suggests that even professional-level courses in physical education may not suffice. One may need classes in commerce and business administration to complement physical education's professional courses. For example, marketing strategy, administrative theory, organizational behavior, and accounting all may have a place in a career of sport planning, programming, and management.

Thus, liberal education lays a foundation for these careers, and courses in physical education together with coursework completed outside the field can serve as building blocks for a degree program.

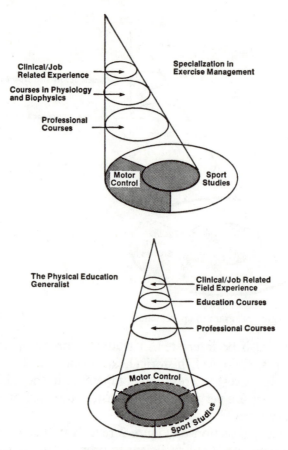

Figure 3. Degree programs for exercise management and teaching.

Assuming that some subject matter applies to a career more than others do, the career choice is easier to make. For instance, interest and competence in sport studies is important for persons choosing related careers.

Figure 3 shows two other examples of career preparation. It depicts the same configurations as Figure 2 with the same assumptions about the importance of liberal education, the need for a common core of performance experiences and analysis courses, and the same need to add courses, like building blocks, in preparing for the career.

Persons interested in careers for exercise prescription and management, then, start from the same foundation as persons interested in other areas. They differ only in the kind of depth and specialization they choose to add to this foundation. Prospective exercise managers may choose specialized performance experiences and courses, and by necessity will gain great mastery over the disciplinary subject matter called motor control. That is, they would seek an understanding of exercise and its effects, which would entail the study of human performance from physiological, anatomical, mechanical, and neurological perspectives. Why? Because people wishing to pursue a career of prescribing exercises for others must possess a thorough knowledge of exercise and what it will and will not accomplish under what conditions. Just as interest and competency in sport studies was deemed important for people in sport management, programming, and planning, so must people interested in exercise management have the same interest and aptitude toward motor control. Its presence or absence indicates whether this career choice is appropriate.

Persons in exercise management also need professional-level courses in physical education such as principles of training and conditioning, stress management, and the design of exercise programs. They need significant field experiences. Furthermore, they may need coursework outside physical education such as in nutrition and human physiology.

Figure 3 also suggests the kind of preparation that may be appropriate for teachers and coaches. Unlike the other two examples, which are by nature more specialized, teachers and coaches require a solid but more generalized background. Their specialization is revealed partly in the breadth of their study, both in performance and performance analysis.

The other part of their specialization follows the same concept as in two careers. Teachers and coaches need numerous professional-level courses in physical education in teaching methodology, curriculum design, and analysis of teaching and coaching behaviors, in addition to appropriate field experiences. They will have to complete coursework in education as part of the certification process so vital in teaching. As in careers of exercise management and sport programming, students must have a basic interest and must develop competence in the necessary subject matter. In fact, the very nature of teaching and coaching require a breadth of experience and understanding nearly unparalleled by other careers in physical education. Persons interested in this career should enjoy performing and analyzing performance, especially as it enhances the learning and performance capabilities of students and athletes.

These three examples illustrate how courses in physical education and those outside it can be building blocks for a career. In each case, the principles and assumptions are essentially the same; a direct relationship exists between the subject matter one masters and the career requirements he or she anticipates. Hence, even where formal degree programs do not exist in physical education, it is usually possible for individuals to plan for a career by giving close attention to the kind and sequencing of the courses they elect. Moreover, an important way to learn about a career is to begin preparation for it. There is really no substitute for direct experience.

Learning More about the Responsibilities and Demands of a Career

Another crucial part of choosing a career is to probe the alternatives. Textbooks give only partial clues about the "real" situation, so it is important to see firsthand how the work is performed and how it changes.

This change should be expected. Many of today's professionals completed their undergraduate education prior to the 1960s. We have established that the way one's work is performed today may not be the way it should be performed tomorrow; and people find it difficult to behave in new ways when they have not received appropriate education and training. In this sense, your analysis of the way work is performed requires you to have two qualities: compassion and imagination. Compassion helps you understand how the work is defined and performed, and imagination helps you consider what the career might become.

The fact remains that if you are seeking a realistic career choice, merely reading about careers will not suffice. You will need to enter the workplace and ask people who perform the work about its essentials, benefits, and disadvantages. A single excursion is not enough. Just as tourists miss a great deal as they move from place to place, so will students making brief visits to gymnasia and other agencies see just a part of the work that may ultimately be their own.

Instead, one should employ related measures for a thorough acquaintance with this work. If extensive observation is possible, for example, one could observe different practitioners in the various agencies. Not all practitioners are the same, nor are the demands in one agency necessarily the same in others. Thus, a broad sampling provides the best picture of each type of work.

The other measure is to talk with practitioners, people who are actually performing the work and who are, after all, your potential colleagues in the profession. Most will take the time to discuss their career with you, and their candor often is both informative and refreshing. A list of questions you may want to use for these interviews appears in Table 3. These questions have been field tested with persons in various careers and are offered here as examples of how to initiate discussion. They are structured to tap difference of opinion on many matters in the profession. The responses you get should help clarify your career choice, particularly where no specialized degree program exists at your college or university. Remember, many careers are so new that one should gather information from every possible source in order to make the best career choice.

The Tension between Career Preparation and Practice

Understanding the requirements for work in a given career can help you make a choice; yet a tension exists between career preparation in higher education and the way some practitioners define and perform their work. This tension exists because of the difference between theory and practice, or in other words, the difference between education and training. A student can take either of two possible orientations, role-taking or role-making, as presented in the introduction. Let's explore this issue.

All professional degree programs must prepare students to perform work as it is currently defined and conducted—for two good reasons. The first, and most obvious, is that new graduates will not have any impact on the profession or on society unless they are hired; and to be hired, they must be able to do the work that the hiring agencies require. A second reason is that many excellent practitioners today not only perform their work with distinction, but they also are good models to imitate. That is, certain forms of knowledge, sensitivity, and skill are best learned from master practitioners who already possess them in the work world. This is true in physical education as much as in other professions.

With both of these reasons in mind, designers of professional preparation programs often list characteristics, competencies, and behaviors appropriate for each given career. This list guides course construction and sets a standard against which students may gauge

Table 3
Examples of Questions to Ask Practitioners

1. How long have you been in this job? Who set the requirements for it? How much power do you have in determining how you perform your job? Approximately how many hours per week do you spend on the job? How do you apportion your time?

2. How adequate was your preparation in higher education for your work role? What were the major strengths of your professional education? What were the major weaknesses? In your view, what is the ideal relationship between higher education and the work organization? What responsibilities are linked to each agency?

3. What degree(s) do you possess? Are you currently working toward an advanced degree? Are you currently involved in a form of continuing education or professional development? Why, or why not?

4. If you had the responsibility of hiring people to perform your work, what would you look for in the candidates for your job?

5. In the course of your work, have you identified some questions or problems that require research? What are they? Have you tried to communicate them to researchers?

6. How do you know when you are successful in your work? What criteria do you use? What are the major barriers to your effectiveness?

7. Are you a member of a professional association? Do you receive professional journals? How much time do you have for reading and staying abreast of new developments in your field?

8. How helpful is the research literature in the performance of your role? In what ways should research be communicated to practitioners like you?

9. Is it possible for someone in your job to become obsolete professionally? What are the causes? What are the remedies?

10. Have you ever tried to construct a model of how you think about, and actually perform, your work? How successful were you? Have you evaluated this model since you constructed it?

11. Are you under the supervision of another professional? Are you satisfied with the quantity and quality of supervision? What criteria are used to evaluate your effectiveness?

12. What are your views on the needs and problems of your clients (students)? Can you identify types or groups of clients?

13. To what extent does your professional life affect your personal life? Do you encounter conflicts between different parts of your job?

14. Do you see yourself in this same job 5 years from now? Ten years from now? Explain. What will the future bring for jobs like yours?

15. List the questions you would like to ask.

their progress. Clearly, all members of the profession must strive to insure that tomorrow's graduates will be able to perform work. There is no tension here between theory and practice.

The tension arises when people who design career preparation programs structure courses and experiences that depart from current work roles. Whether this departure is slight or dramatic, the same fundamental tension is created because the message is that things are not what they could be, or should be, in the work world. This is a value judgment, and like all value judgments it fosters differences of opinion. Such opposing views are evident in the negative evaluations some practitioners give to professional education programs, as well as in the resistance some students have to courses and experiences that, in their view, depart dramatically from their chosen role. Frequently both students and practitioners say, "It's just too theoretical." They perhaps mean that the knowledge, sensitivities, and skills have little relevance to work in the field today. Their judgments often are correct—these new approaches will not work unless they represent real changes in the way work is defined, performed, and evaluated.

Here, then, is the source of the tension: Programs of professional or career preparation have a dual obligation, which their designers try to meet. They endeavor to prepare students for work roles as they currently exist, yet *at the same time* hope to prepare them for the anticipated changes in these roles. Meeting this obligation requires the appreciation and understanding of all persons in the profession, especially students.

In some respects, two types of preparation mirror the differences between education and training. If professional preparation programs were designed exclusively to follow practice, then much training and only a little education would result. But virtually every program in physical education seeks to prepare people for future roles. In so doing, their courses are designed to offer appropriate and valuable professional training as well as professional education that will accommodate change. Remember, training and education are related and compatible, yet different. Thus, a first-rate professional education program should actively seek both. The educated professional is trained to meet today's demands and responsibilities as well as tomorrow's challenges.

At a more personal level, this tension in career preparation can be understood in relation to role-taking and role-making. Although it is important that all persons in the profession come to grips with their personal orientation in this regard, it is pivotal for students who are planning a career. The quality and composition of the professional education program for a role-taker will differ significantly from that for a role-maker, and so will their requirements for courses and related experiences vary, as illustrated by the following contrast.

Role-takers assume there is a best way to define and perform work, and that this way will not change for a long time. Role-makers, however, assume there are a number of different ways to perform the same work, and that these ways may change over time. Role-takers assume that all agencies (e.g., all schools and their programs) are basically alike, so that what works in one will work in the others. In contrast, role-makers assume that even agencies of the same kind (e.g., schools) differ significantly, and therefore, that role-makers must receive a broad education to help them choose an appropriate strategy for each situation. Role-takers expect professional education programs and researchers to follow practice, whereas role-makers expect some leadership from programs and researchers. Role-takers seek largely the vocational training necessary to have a job. Role-makers seek, in addition to training, the professional education that is part of a career. These contrasting orientations hold true for teaching, coaching, and work in the other physical education careers that are so important to the profession's future.

Thus, the tension between professional education and practice can be identified in any college or university at two levels. It exists in the design of professional education programs that target both present and future work performance, and exists in the way students, faculty, and practitioners orient themselves toward role-taking or role-making.

This tension is not unique to physical education; it has been discussed in relation to a number of professions (Glazer, 1974). It stems from balancing professions between their current effectiveness and their need to respond to a changing society. The challenge of keeping the proper balance rests with every member of the profession. Students deciding which careers to pursue must understand this tension and the possible orientations toward it in order to eventually meet physical education's high standards of professionalism.

Summary

Earlier in the history of the profession, students majoring in physical education were prepared only for teaching-coaching roles in schools, colleges, and universities. Today this is no longer true. Although careers in teaching and coaching remain central to physical education, alternatives also exist for careers other than teaching and agencies other than schools, colleges, and universities. Consequently, students in physical education have a *bona fide* choice of careers in connection with their undergraduate major.

Students should begin career planning soon after entering higher education. They should confront a series of personal questions, and complete an inventory of the appropriate career opportunities and the professional education needed for these careers. They should consider the nature of the work and how it is defined and evaluated. Such career-specific information helps in choosing among the alternatives and in planning a degree program. Yet, career planning should also include broader questions regarding one's own preferences about lifestyle.

Some institutions may not have formal degree programs for selected alternative careers. In these instances, it is nevertheless possible to plan an appropriate degree program in physical education if, after the field work requirements are determined, students use the appropriate courses in physical education as building blocks toward their chosen career. Indeed, students' interests and competence in certain portions of the field's subject matter may be decisive factors in choosing a career. After all, this subject matter must be mastered in professional preparation before being applied in the work world. In the profession of physical education, a direct relationship exists between the knowledge and skill mastered in professional education and how the work is defined and performed.

On the other hand, tensions exist between professional education and practice at two levels. Programs of professional education attempt to prepare students for meeting the work demands of today and yet accommodate to changes in the future. Therefore not all coursework will directly apply to the immediate demands of practice, and the mere fact that such a discrepancy exists causes some tension among members of the profession.

Tension also exists in the different orientations of individuals in the profession, including students. Some orient themselves toward role-taking, others toward role-making. Role-takers and role-makers hold different assumptions and approaches to work, with their expectations affecting the organization, conduct, and effectiveness of professional education programs.

A balance must be maintained at both levels if the profession is to remain viable. Every member in the profession must understand the importance of this balance and act to maintain it. This responsibility begins when students choose a career, start planning for it, and undertake appropriate professional education and training, and it continues throughout their careers.

Supplementary Activities

Self-testing Exercises

After reading chapter 6, you should be able to:

1. Begin the process of choosing a career, or reaffirm your choice;
2. Identify the sources to consult as part of career planning;
3. Discuss the ways in which courses in physical education can serve as building blocks toward your career.
4. Identify coursework outside physical education that is appropriate for your career.
5. Discuss the tensions between professional education and practice, as well as between role-taking and role-making, and formulate a personal point of view on these related matters.

Class Activities

1. Using the questions in Table 3, interview professionals in physical education who perform different kinds of work. Then develop career profiles for the different kinds of careers. In so doing, look for similarities and differences in the same jobs, as well as across jobs. Finally, discuss whether all of these people are part of the profession of physical education. If they are not now, should they be?
2. Interview other students and faculty in physical education to determine whether they lean more toward role-making or role-taking. Then find out about the courses in physical education. Which ones are directed toward present work demands, and

which ones are directed toward the future? Which ones are appropriate for any career? Only for specific careers?

Questions for Discussion

1. What do practitioners in the work world think about their jobs? What kind of preparation for these jobs do they deem necessary? Do you agree?
2. In addition to those identified, what careers might persons like you *create* in the near future? Can you envision specialized degree programs in higher education for these careers?
3. Are all persons who seek the various careers in the field part of the same profession, or do they form many different professions? What are the implications of your answer.
4. Can you think of ways in which persons in the various careers might begin to cooperate in order to provide better service to society? For example, should there be a relationship between the school physical education teacher, the physical fitness consultant, and the community recreation leader? Explain.
5. What are the safeguards against obsolescence in your chosen career?

Sources for Additional Reading

BRYANT, J. The year 2001 AD and future careers in physical education. *The Physical Educator*, 1979, **36**(4), 197-200.

CONSIDINE, W.J. (Ed.). *Alternative professional preparation in physical education*. Washington, DC: AAHPERD, 1979.

LAMBERT, C. What can I do besides teach? *Journal of Physical Education, Recreation, and Dance*, 1980, **51**(9), 74-76.

LAWSON, H.A. (Ed.). *Undergraduate education: Issues and approaches*. Washington, DC: AAHPERD, 1981.

MEYERSON, M. Civilizing education: Uniting liberal and professional learning. *Daedalus*, 1974, **103**(4), 173-189.

SAGEN, H.B. Careers, competencies, and liberal education. *Liberal Education*, 1979, **65**(2), 150-166.

PART 3

A profession is a special kind of occupation, and the profession of physical education is special because of the nature of its work and the preparation for it. In both cases, a specialized body of knowledge, sensitivities, and skills is central to the livelihood of the profession.

The *knowledge system* in physical education refers to the profession's ways of generating, organizing, transporting, communicating, and using its knowledge, sensitivities, and skills. This knowledge system affects everyone in the profession, and so everyone is responsible for knowledge about it and involvement in it. On the other hand, different kinds of people play equally different kinds of roles in this system. Some create new knowledge, others organize and transport it, and others will only consume it. These different roles are complementary, much like the complementary relationship that exists among specialized members of the same athletic team. Each requires the other if the team or the profession's knowledge system is to be successful.

The parts of physical education's knowledge system and their relationship are presented in Part 3. Knowledge generation and the functions of inquiry are presented in chapter 7. The organization or packaging of knowledge so generated is discussed in chapter 8, with ways to transport and communicate this knowledge following in chapter 9. Factors that facilitate, inhibit, and prohibit the use of knowledge in practice are identified in chapter 10, and the uses of knowledge for lifelong learning in the profession are discussed in chapter 11. Together, these chapters illustrate the importance of physical education's knowledge system.

CHAPTER 7
Generating knowledge for the profession

If you plan to pursue a career in physical education, then you must be prepared to accept three major commitments: to serve society, to perform work with distinction while remaining in the profession throughout your working life, and to use new knowledge in your work. This last commitment is in many ways the most important of the three, because only by meeting it can you be assured of providing a societal service and of performing work with distinction. This implies that you must constantly check your progress in relation to all three commitments. To *believe* in them is simply not enough; you must demonstrate these commitments by your *actions*, particularly in using new knowledge to check your progress.

Every member of the profession must therefore try to assimilate new knowledge as it is produced. This means that each must have an understanding of the knowledge system for physical education—how knowledge is generated, organized, transported, and utilized. Without such an understanding, members of the profession who wish to meet the aforementioned commitments would not know where to seek useful knowledge, what to look for, or what standards to employ in assessing it. With such an understanding of the knowledge system, professionals may more easily meet these commitments. Consequently, aspiring professionals must examine the related parts of this knowledge system and the practical ways in which it affects work.

To begin discussion of the knowledge system, let's examine the profession's ways of generating new knowledge. This is a good place to start because if knowledge were not generated continuously, then we would have fewer concerns about its organization, transportation, and use in practice. The fact is, however, that new knowledge is being created at an ever increasing pace, and its use in practice hinges upon one's appreciation and understanding of this process. Such an appreciation and understanding is made easier by considering three related questions. What are the functions of inquiry in physical education? How may this inquiry be categorized, and with what descriptors? What are the methods of generating new knowledge, who uses them, and what kinds of knowledge result from each?

The Functions of Inquiry

Inquiry into any part of life is propelled by human curiosity, with the understanding gained in the process often serving as its own justification. The same is true for many kinds of inquiry in physical education. Investigators become interested in a question because they are curious. The knowledge they gain both during and after their investigations may serve no other need than satisfying their curiosity.

On the other hand, physical education is a professional field, and the kind of knowledge generated usually brings three dividends to the world of practice. Practice is improved, or justified, or changed in a revolutionary way.

Improvement of Practice

The most apparent of these dividends of inquiry is the improvement of work in the profession. Most commonly, the goals or objectives for work are accepted as given, and the most pressing issue is to find the best way of accomplishing them. For example, physical education teachers have accepted the responsibility for helping their students become physically fit; the question thus is not whether teachers should attempt this task, but how best to accomplish it. Moreover, coaches accept as their target the responsibility for maximizing athletes' performance. For these coaches, the question is how to make this happen. One job of athletic trainers is to speed rehabilitation of athletes, the question again being how to proceed. So, a common need in all kinds of work in physical education is to find the best way of meeting one's responsibilities, and formal inquiry often helps the selection, particularly in the following three ways.

First, formal inquiry may accomplish little more than to confirm existing practices. For example, a teacher may find that the methods selected to develop physical fitness are the best available, given the circumstances in the school and the knowledge on hand. This is a worthwhile finding, nevertheless; it improves practice because it offers more formal support for the teacher's approach to work, an approach which in the beginning may have been an educated guess. Moreover, the same teacher eventually might have had doubts about this approach and exchanged it for another, again making only an educated guess. Who knows how long such a process of making educated guesses would have lasted? Such guesswork is a breeding ground for error. Thus, the mere fact that inquiry confirmed the teacher's approach to physical fitness helped to improve work performance. Without such confirmation, this teacher might have wasted time substituting one educated guess for another, and the students might have been less fit as a consequence.

Second, formal inquiry may improve practice by discrediting a professional's methods. For example, a coach interested in maximizing athletes' performance may find that methods used in past situations fail to yield the same results now. Questions arise in this person's mind and stimulate a search of the literature. The coach may discover why the old methods no longer work and may even learn that they were incorrect to begin with. In either case, the published results of inquiry helped to improve coaching practice by initiating the search for new methods. Even if inquiry did not point to these methods, it did indicate what *not* to do, which in itself improves practice.

Third, practice can be improved when inquiry results in a new way of performing work. Such a "new way" in a profession often is called a *technology*, where technology refers to the organization of knowledge and skill for the achievement of practical purposes. The athletic trainer may learn a new way of preventing knee injuries in football, a way discovered by persons studying the incidence and causes of knee injury. The teacher may learn a new way to organize and conduct classes, a technology stemming from inquiry of teacher educators in physical education. Clearly, these technologies are among the most valuable contributions to practice in the profession. As the amount of inquiry increases, there is hope that the number of technologies available also will increase. If so, practice in the profession will improve significantly.

Justification of Practice

The knowledge resulting from inquiry in physical education may also serve to better justify practice. Two scenarios demonstrate the need for physical educators to lend support to their work, as discussed below. With the results from inquiry, practitioners may be able to meet the challenges associated with each scenario. Without such support, these practitioners hold beliefs that are much less secure and defensible. Since the stakes are high in both situations, the advantages of useful inquiry will become apparent.

In the first scenario, practitioners are asked to justify their programs, and consequently their jobs. This happens in all fields, but most frequently in fields depending on public support and funding. For example, why should physical education programs be required of all students in secondary schools? Are the results of physical education worth the expense of conducting the program? As another example, why offer interscholastic athletic programs in schools when opportunities exist for sport in the community and when the school's teams are restricted to only a few athletes?

These questions are rather common and they indicate that many people do not have the same appreciation and understanding for these programs as do professionals in physical education. Both programs and physical educators must be justified. Although personal beliefs and emotions may lend strength when arguing for these programs, they are rarely sufficient in a society where more and more people are becoming highly educated and demanding more sophisticated justification. As part of their defense, therefore, practitioners must cite results from formal inquiry into these programs, including their effects on athletes and students. Conversely, practitioners who want to *expand* their programs also will have to document their reasons with respect to the knowledge generated in physical education. In both examples, the results of inquiry can enrich the justification offered.

The second scenario is becoming increasingly common in all professions and is especially apparent in physical education. Practitioners are being taken to court for their actions or inactions concerning work. Legal battles of this kind are common in physical education because so many kinds of work in the profession involve risks to those being served. For example, a boy falls off a climbing frame in an elementary school program and breaks his neck. His parents file suit against the teacher, charging negligence, and ask $2 million in damages. Or, a gymnast slips off the balance beam, lands on a fixture protruding from the floor, and loses sight in one eye. Her parents sue the coach for $3 million, citing the permanence of the impairment and the need for proper retribution.

When practitioners are placed on trial in situations like these, the burden of proof often is theirs. They must be prepared to justify what they did, documenting the fact that their actions or inactions were consistent with the existing state of knowledge in the profession. Here again, the knowledge gained from inquiry and used in practice provides an important justification for performing work a certain way. Membership in a profession implies expertise, and the results of inquiry form the basis for this expertise.

Revolutionary Changes in Practice

The results from an inquiry may cause a revolutionary change in practice, a change in which the actual goals and structure of a program are altered. These changes may vary in degrees and kinds, as the following two examples illustrate, but they are nonetheless major.

One revolutionary change has been in the subject matter and purposes of school physical education. Although these programs were almost exclusively activity-based in the past, they are now being altered in many schools as a direct result of knowledge generated in physical education. Practitioners formerly had assumed that students would derive a number of benefits simply by participating in physical and ludic activities, benefits including sportsmanship, knowledge about sport in society, and health and fitness. Unfortunately, investigation into the school programs did not confirm these claims. It became clear that if these outcomes were to be achieved, then education about performance in physical and ludic activities would have to be added to the school curriculum. Some people called the approach "basic stuff," others called it a "concept curriculum," and still others called it a "disciplinary approach" because knowledge from the discipline Franklin Henry had envisioned was being offered to students in the schools. Mastery of this subject matter was added as a goal of the program, recasting the roles of teacher and student in the process. Although this type of program is not evident in every school district, it shows how inquiry can result in major change.

A second example of revolutionary change in the field ties into discussions from earlier chapters. The missions and subject matter for physical education have changed dramatically through knowledge generated in the profession. Where the profession was once limited to teacher-coaches in schools, it now includes a range of professionals who work in numerous agencies. Where it once relied on the school to serve all of society, it now uses a more comprehensive approach. The disciplinary movement was mainly responsible for this revolutionary change, so it is no coincidence that this movement was based on the need to generate a more diversified and comprehensive knowledge base.

These, then, are just two recent examples of how efforts to generate knowledge resulted in major, revolutionary changes in the field's practical operations. Such restructuring of missions and goals affects every other part of practice. Therefore, this function of formal inquiry in physical education is just as important as the other two. Change, after all, paves the way for future work in the profession, a future that will reflect the present course of inquiry.

Kinds of Inquiry

Different types of inquiry in physical education have different import for practice. Some are more likely to improve practice, while others help to justify or change it. This will become clearer as we introduce four kinds of inquiry to assist you in identifying and categorizing each.

Search Versus Research

Thus far in the discussion, the word *research* has not been used although it has been implied. Instead, the descriptors used were "inquiry" and "generation of knowledge." The reason for this selective use of terms is that a difference exists between a *search* and the subsequent *re-search*; the latter suggests a return to familiar territory, whereas the former implies pioneering work on the frontiers of knowledge. Both are important in physical education, as is the distinction between them, and yet they enjoy a special relationship.

The importance of the *search* in physical education's inquiry stems from the newness of the field. Whereas mathematics, chemistry, and history are centuries old, physical education does not have such a long heritage of inquiry; this brings different challenges for the profession's investigators. Whereas investigators in other fields endeavor to answer enduring questions, their colleagues in physical education often face the task of *identifying appropriate questions*. New questions signal the *search* for truth at the frontiers of knowledge. This activity is vital in all fields because the questions asked will determine the answers received, these answers ultimately becoming what members of the profession call knowledge.

Once the search is well underway, as revealed by identifying appropriate questions and providing tentative explanations, the process of *research* begins. By definition, research involves a repeat performance. Scholars involved in research address an enduring question to determine if the answers that have been accepted are complete and accurate. They may try to replicate the work of others by adopting the same methods in the same circumstances, or they may choose a different way to get at the same question. Either way, their efforts are valuable for they may confirm earlier work or pave the way for additional work. Research is thus additive and integrative in physical education.

So even though the two are different, a direct relationship exists between the search and subsequent research in physical education.

They provide two, complementary approaches to mapping the field's knowledge. The search gives the clues to the heretofore unknown, while the repeated research that follows provides greater detail and certainty. In short, the quality of research depends upon the quality of the search. Thus, the search is crucial in physical education even though it may not have an immediate effect upon practice; this leads to a second category for inquiry.

Basic Versus Applied Inquiry

When the questions an investigator chooses to study have no apparent bearing upon the current realities of practice—often the case with a search—the investigator is said to be engaged in *basic inquiry*. Basic inquiry is a quest for knowledge and understanding with no obvious and immediate application to work in the profession. It contrasts with applied inquiry, which by definition is conducted for use in practice and may function to improve, justify, or change practice in an immediate, direct way.

Persons involved with basic inquiry often are viewed in the "ivory tower" image. Although this may be understandable in an applied, professional field, it is somewhat of a misconception about basic inquiry and those who choose to undertake it. Consider the future: In 20 years what is now basic research may have resulted in a wealth of new knowledge serving to improve, justify, and even change practice! Human physiology is a case in point. The first attempts at understanding physiology hundreds of years ago were at the time examples of basic inquiry. Today, the knowledge about physiology is vast and it includes exercise physiology, which is immensely useful to practice in physical education. This applied knowledge of the present day would not have developed without basic inquiry. Thus, basic inquiry holds the promise of longer-term dividends whereas applied inquiry's dividends are immediate.

Descriptive-Explanatory Versus Prescriptive Inquiry

Inquiry may serve no other purpose than to inform members of the profession about aspects of their work. Structured this way, inquiry is said to be descriptive-explanatory because its aim is to describe and explain things about work. For example, some investigators in physical education try to determine why students exposed to one teaching method learn the same skill differently than students exposed to another method. Or perhaps investigators wish to learn about the effects of yoga on a participant's physical fitness and psychological characteristics. In both cases the intent is to at least describe the outcomes and maybe even explain them. An investigator may ultimately be able to make predictions about what will happen under similar circumstances. Like a successful gambler, the investigator who has enough descriptive-explanatory information is in a position to bet on a prediction.

To describe, explain, and predict, however, is not to *prescribe*. Descriptive information tells the reader *about* something, not what to do to it. In contrast, prescriptive inquiry seeks the best ways to accomplish parts of work, and it may produce a useful technology. For example, trying to determine the best way of teaching tennis to eighth-grade students is prescriptive inquiry, as is seeking how to organize and conduct an athletics program. The results tell practitioners what to do in each case.

Here too, the profession needs both processes because the adequacy of prescriptive inquiry depends largely on having adequate descriptive-explanatory information. In other words, the more we know about something (from descriptive-explanatory inquiry), the easier it is to know what to do about it (from prescriptive inquiry). If an investigator wants to do prescriptive research to help school physical education teachers improve their methods, a prerequisite understanding about the realities of teaching physical education must be gained from descriptive-explanatory inquiry. Moreover, if a physiologist wants to tell an exercise leader how to change a senior citizen's behavior (prescriptive inquiry), he or she must be informed about the behavior and physiological characteristics of senior citizens (which stem from descriptive-explanatory inquiry). These two kinds of inquiry thus are complementary in a profession such as physical education.

Normative Versus Nonnormative Inquiry

A norm is a standard or value, and hence one can distinguish between kinds of inquiry based on the presence or absence of norms accepted in advance by the investigator. *Normative inquiry* is colored by such a standard or value, whereas *nonnormative in-*

quiry proceeds without such a standard. In physical education, normative research is designed to show that parts of work are good; nonnormative inquiry is designed to examine what is there, quite apart from making a value judgment.

Consider a researcher who is interested in psychological concerns such as personality, attitude, and motivation in physical and ludic activities, for example. If this person were to assume a normative posture, it would be apparent in many ways, beginning with the title of the work. A title such as "Psychological Benefits of Participation in Physical and Ludic Activities" is not neutral. It shows that the investigator is looking only for *benefits*, and also suggests that he or she has assumed in advance that such participation is good. From start to finish, the investigation has been rigged to produce only those findings the investigator wanted to uncover. This is normative inquiry.

By contrast, consider an example of nonnormative inquiry. Here the title would be something like "Psychological Effects of Participation in Physical and Ludic Activities." The investigator's intention is simply: Let me see what I shall uncover. The potential effects may be found to be detrimental, beneficial, or inconsequential, but this will not be known until after the investigation is completed. Finally, the investigator may not even make judgments about whether the results are good or bad, instead leaving that task to those reading the study.

Thus, the differences between normative and nonnormative inquiry affect the kind of knowledge at the profession's disposal. Although professional physical educators champion human involvement in physical and ludic activity, their use of normative inquiry to prove its worth has shortcomings. Inquiry guided by these beliefs will result in knowledge that is selectively filtered through the values of the investigator, who will not allow negative or unintended outcomes. This is why nonnormative inquiry is so important; unlike normative inquiry, it allows detection of unwanted and unintended outcomes. After all, if negative outcomes are to be eliminated they must first be identified. Nonnormative inquiry, thus valuable in physical education, is practiced by different kinds of investigators who use different methods to generate equally different kinds of knowledge.

Methods for Generating Knowledge

Investigators, methods, and knowledge can be categorized in many ways. In the interests of simplicity and clarity, however, only three categories are presented here.

Scientific Inquiry

Knowledge about human involvement in physical and ludic activities, and about the behavior of teachers, coaches, and other kinds of professionals in physical education, is gained through scientific inquiry. The persons performing this inquiry are called scientists and their results may be called *scientific knowledge.*

Science provides a system of gaining knowledge that is applicable to many fields of study, including physical education. As McCain and Segal (1973) suggest, science is like a game. Scientists in physical education who choose to play this game abide by a clearly defined set of rules and principles. The object of the game is to produce a special kind of knowledge called scientific knowledge, which results when scientists play the game by its rules as determined by their colleagues who act as referees. Indeed, the scientists publish their work in *refereed* journals, meaning these works must pass review by a jury of peers to insure quality in science.

The rules for the game of science include experimentation, the ability to manipulate and control some of the things being studied and, perhaps most of all, the ability of the scientist to observe directly and to assess the results from the experiment. It is in publishing these results that the significance of scientific research becomes apparent, for after reading the work of a colleague, a scientist elsewhere should be able to duplicate the same study and get the same findings. It makes little difference what has been studied, because every part of the scientific enterprise is supposed to be made public and testable. This is the way the game is played.

Other parts of the game explain how scientific knowledge results. The scientist begins with hypotheses, or educated guesses. When hypotheses are confirmed, the scientist then claims to have facts, which form the basis for sentences called propositions. For example, a study on the effects of little league competition on preadolescent boys revealed that they valued winning at all costs over fair play. From this result the scientist drew a proposition: The greater the frequency and intensity of sport involvement among preadolescent children, the greater the likelihood that they will substitute winning at all costs for orientations such as having fun and playing fairly. A proposition such as this gives rise to hypotheses for the investigations of the future. A future hypothesis could be: Preadolescent girls involved in little league competition will value winning at all costs over other possible outcomes. "If this, then that" is the rule of thumb in constructing propositions.

Interrelated propositions are then grouped together in a theory. The proposition about preadolescent children in the preceding example is just one of many required for a theory of sport involvement. All such theories are constructed by scientists and their purpose is to describe, explain and, where possible, predict events and behaviors. As organizational devices that integrate similar research from the past and help direct the scientist's thinking, theories are reviewed continuously and revised where necessary. Sometimes they are discarded, especially when a competing theory seems superior in describing, explaining, and predicting. In other words, a theory's value depends on how well it corresponds to reality. Thus, nothing is so practical as good theory. When people say "it's too theoretical," they really should modify the statement to: "I question the adequacy of this theory." Scientific theories are grounded in reality and accordingly are called *grounded theories*.

Occasionally, well developed and verified theories become *laws*, which identify unchanging relationships among things, such as Newton's laws of motion. Yet laws are rare in science and are even more rare in new fields of inquiry such as physical education. Laws in physical education are, at this point, borrowed from other fields. Aside from Newton's laws, applied to the biomechanics of performance, some physiological laws are used in research on performance at high altitudes and under water. Although new laws may surface in the future, most scientists in physical education currently are working to develop, test, and revise theories. This enterprise constitutes a career opportunity to which some readers are invited.

Scholarly Inquiry

Scientific inquiry generates important scientific knowledge in physical education; this inquiry is one way of generating knowledge, but not the only way. Likewise, scientists constitute one group of investigators—not the only group—and scientific knowledge is only one kind of knowledge in physical education. These observations do not diminish the importance of scientific inquiry. They simply alert members of the profession to other ways of knowing, to people other than scientists who use these ways, and to different kinds of knowledge. Returning to our metaphor, the game of science is just one of many possible games that members of the profession may play in order to generate new knowledge.

Scholarly inquiry is employed here as a catch-all category for formal inquiry that meets many of the same requirements as scientific inquiry. Scholars are those who engage in this inquiry, and the knowledge they produce may be called *scholarly knowledge*. This definition suggests that scholars often are removed from the demands of practice in the profession for, like scientists, scholars must undergo long, rigorous, formal education and training in order to generate knowledge. The major difference between the work of scholars and scientists is that scholarly inquiry does not always require the design of an experiment, the ability to manipulate and control the things being studied, or the ability to directly observe and assess the effects of the experiment. Thus, scientific inquiry usually includes quantitative measures, whereas scholarly inquiry involves qualitative assessments.

Examples of scholarly inquiry, scholars who perform it, and the scholarly knowledge they generate are numerous in physical education. Scholars who conduct historical investigations and philosophical analyses are among the most obvious, but many others contribute as well. Harper (1982), for example, cites the importance of popular fiction as a messenger of truth; novels reveal interesting findings about people, findings that do not lend themselves to scientific inquiry. In addition, studying some forms of art appropriately can yield valuable understanding about human involvement in physical and ludic activities. Furthermore, a detailed analysis of the roles and goals of school physical education programs is a scholarly task resulting in scholarly knowledge.

A special kind of theory may even result from scholarly knowledge, called a *normative theory*. Unlike the scientist's grounded theory that describes reality, a scholar's *normative theory* suggests what programs and society should resemble in the ideal sense. In other words, normative theory resulting from scholarly knowledge sets a standard that members in the profession may work toward. And like normative inquiry, normative theory reflects the investigator's values.

Thus, scholarly knowledge may be descriptive and explanatory as well as prescriptive, nonnormative as well as normative. It results from many forms of qualitative inquiry, the common objective being to increase knowledge in a field. It is based on the assumption that scientific inquiry, with its requirement for direct observation and quantification, cannot reveal everything we seek to know about humans. These qualitative forms of scholarly inquiry often are called humanistic because they are founded on the need to understand what it means to be human. Accordingly, the results they produce—the scholarly knowledge—constitute part of the humanities. This kind of work is relatively new in physical education but it has already made an impact on the field. Scholarly inquiry promises to become even more important in the future as the appreciation of its value increases and more scholars are prepared for this work.

Reflective Inquiry

The third method of generating knowledge in physical education is *reflective inquiry*. Although this label is new, the form of inquiry is as old as humanity. People reflect regularly on their thoughts and experiences, and they learn from this process. The same technique works for performers and practitioners in physical education. For example, a teacher asks why one student learned so much while another did not. A coach ponders why a strategy worked against one opponent but not against the other. A tennis player reflects back on the first set in preparation for the second. Examples are numerous of practitioners and performers in physical education who commonly engage in reflective inquiry; their results may be called *experiential knowledge*, a term emphasizing the role of personal experience in this process.

For the most part, neither practitioners nor performers have received the long, rigorous, formal training demanded of scientists and scholars. Therefore, they are producing a different kind of knowledge, one forged out of personal and direct experiences but not necessarily generated according to strict rules of inquiry. The resulting knowledge is not less valuable than scientific or scholarly results; it is simply different and must be evaluated and used accordingly. The two examples below illustrate the uses and importance of experiential knowledge.

A ski instructor faces the task of improving performance skills of beginning, intermediate, and advanced skiers. Scientific knowledge may help the instructor determine the proper progression in instruction, the kinds of performance errors to expect, and the signs of fatigue to look for. But when the instructor deals with intermediate and advanced skiers, students with high expectations and special needs for instruction, scholarly and scientific knowledge often is not enough. When instructed in a new technique, these students will ask, "What does it feel like?" or, "How will I know when to use this?" The answers to these questions are not easily found in textbooks. To answer them, the instructor must have actually experienced the techniques and reflected upon this experience. The experiential knowledge from this reflection allows the instructor to fill in gaps between scientific and scholarly knowledge. For this reason, a reflective performer often is the best kind of instructor.

As another example, a physical education teacher decides to teach the martial arts to seventh-grade students. Because this teacher is interested in giving them the best possible instruction, he or she consults the related literature. But since so few teachers have ever tried to teach the martial arts to students of this age, and since investigators in physical education have not shown an interest in the question, the teacher finds little help in the scientific and scholarly literature. What is this person to do? One solution is that the teacher, having gained a great deal of experience with seventh-grade students, can use the fruits of this experience to plan instruction—if he or she has engaged in reflective inquiry. Practitioners and performers alike can be more effective in their work if they cultivate and harvest experiential knowledge.

Reflective inquiry in physical education is important and necessary for two reasons. First, knowledge about work and performance must be derived in part from direct experiences. Second, scientific and scholarly knowledge are always, to some extent, incomplete and selective; that is, inquiry emantes from a particular point of view and is part of an endless catch up game. Therefore, whether one is doing work or performing in physical and ludic activities, reflective inquiry is critical for generating the experiential knowledge invaluable to all members of the profession. In fact, the challenge in the years ahead may well be one of formally preparing both performers and practitioners for reflective inquiry. Indeed, later chapters of this text will identify ways in which you can become prepared for this reflective inquiry.

Summary

New knowledge is being generated at an ever increasing pace and professionals must try to assimilate it, which requires an appreciation and understanding of inquiry in physical education. Inquiry in physical education may be pursued for its own sake, where its only purpose may be to satisfy the investigator's curiosity. But three major functions of inquiry in the profession of physical education are improving practice, justifying practice, and occasionally creating revolutionary change in practice.

With these outcomes in mind, members of the profession should acknowledge the need for different kinds of inquiry—for the search as well as research, basic as well as applied inquiry, inquiry that describes and explains as well as prescribes, and nonnormative as well as normative inquiry.

Examples of normative and nonnormative inquiry are apparent in physical education. Although normative inquiry is somewhat justified, it is nonnormative inquiry that paves the way for a truly professional practice because it more accurately depicts what is and is not happening in work. Other kinds of inquiry in physical education also are necessary, and an understanding of the distinctions involved helps the user know what to expect from the study. In this light, the search as part of basic inquiry may grant the beginnings of a description, an explanation, and perhaps a prediction, but it will not tell practitioners what to do. At best, this kind of inquiry will only tell what not to do, or will provide a new understanding that forms the basis for an educated guess.

On the other hand, applied research for prescriptive purposes has immediate uses. Although it is informed by descriptive-explanatory inquiry, it provides direct guidelines to practitioners in physical education. The value of applied, prescriptive inquiry probably will increase in the future, but this fact should not overshadow the need for inquiry of other kinds. Applied, prescriptive inquiry functions primarily to improve and help justify practice. But the more dramatic changes that may be required in the future will most likely stem from the basic, descriptive-explanatory searches of today. Thus, if all three functions of inquiry in the profession are to be achieved, its members must acknowledge the need for different kinds of inquiry along with the different methods each requires.

A variety of different methods exists for generating knowledge in physical education, and several potential categories describe them. For the sake of clarity and simplicity, these may be called scientific inquiry, scholarly inquiry, and reflective inquiry. These methods, used by scientists, scholars, and practitioners or performers, also yield different kinds of knowledge — scientific, scholarly, and experiential knowledge, all of which are important to the profession. Moreover, all are incomplete to some degree and are gathered selectively. Consequently, when the question of who has true knowledge of a subject or practice in physical education is being debated, it is helpful to know what kind of knowledge is being offered, and how it was generated and by whom. Only then can professionals make the informed judgments demonstrating that they perform their work with distinction.

Supplementary Activities

Self-testing Exercises

After reviewing chapter 7, you should be able to:

1. Define the knowledge system for physical education and give its importance;
2. Identify the functions of inquiry in physical education and cite examples of each;

3. Distinguish between inquiry that is: normative and nonnormative; descriptive-explanatory and prescriptive; basic and applied; and, part of the search or the research.
4. Distinguish between grounded theory and normative theory.
5. Identify three ways to generate knowledge, along with the people in the profession who use these ways and the kinds of knowledge they generate.
6. Discuss the importance and uses of scientific, scholarly, and experiential knowledge.

Class Activities

1. Using *Completed Research in Health, Physical Education, and Recreation,* or *The Sport and Recreation Index,* select titles that fall under each of the following categories: search, research, normative, non-normative, basic, applied, descriptive-explanatory, and prescriptive. Pool the results in class. Discuss the results, using questions such as: Which kind of inquiry was easiest to locate? Which was the most difficult? Is the title a good way to make a classification? Which kinds of inquiry are most prevalent in physical education? Why? Is this a good thing? What kinds of changes do you recommend?
2. Examples abound of inquiry into the work of teachers and coaches. Locate some examples in the library. What kinds of inquiry are found here? Is there inquiry into careers other than teaching and coaching? What kind is it? How useful is it?

Questions for Discussion

1. What are the limitations and advantages associated with experiential knowledge, and scholarly and scientific knowledge? Which would you choose and why?
2. Should the textbooks in physical education include experiential knowledge? Do some books already include this kind of knowledge? How do you know whether the contents of a text stem from reflective inquiry or one of the other forms? Are there examples of experiential knowledge in the preceding pages of this text?
3. Are there scientists and scholars on your faculty? How do you

know? What kinds of work do they do? What preparation is required for this work?
4. Is it possible for scientific knowledge to be "too theoretical"? Explain.
5. Is it desirable for practitioners to remain abreast of any new knowledge generated? Is it possible? How can it be done?

Sources for Additional Reading

LOCKE, L.F. *Research in physical education.* New York: Teachers College Press, 1969.

McCAIN, G., & Segal, M. *The game of science.* Monterey, CA: Brooks-Cole, 1973.

SPORT art: Spectacle or sacrament? *Journal of Physical Education, Recreation, and Dance*, 1982, **53**(2), 27-39.

Philosophy
of
Sport

Physiology
of
Sport

Biomechanics
of
Sport

Physical
Education
Profession

Psychology
of
Sport

Sociology
of
Sport

History
of
Sport

CHAPTER 8
The organization of knowledge for the profession

Generating knowledge is the first part of a knowledge system for physical education, and the profession's way of organizing this knowledge constitutes an important second part. New knowledge cannot simply lie around in a profession; it must be used. And its use depends partly on appropriate packaging and labeling. In this sense, new knowledge for physical education is like a new consumer product. After the product has been created, its manufacturer must locate an appropriate market with the right consumers. Then the product must be packaged and labeled accordingly to insure that it meets current demands. So it is with new knowledge. Once created, the appropriate consumers must be identified and the knowledge organized, complete with an appropriate label. These measures help insure that those who seek this knowledge will be able to find it and use it.

Although new knowledge is like a new consumer product in some ways, it is different in others. Most importantly, new knowledge must be blended with existing knowledge; it does not stand apart as a new product. And, the relationship between the organization of knowledge and its generation is significant because the way a profession organizes its knowledge influences the ways in which it is generated. This is so because the people who generate knowledge organize themselves under the same labels as the knowledge itself, and their inquiry is framed accordingly.

For example, if some knowledge is organized under the label "psychology of sport," the persons who generate this knowledge will call themselves "sport psychologists," their inquiry will follow the lead of psychology, and their knowledge will be shared with other sport psychologists in journals and books that bear a label such as Sport Psychology or Psychology of Sport. Similarly, if knowledge is organized under the label "physical education," it will determine who generates this knowledge, the questions they address, and the journals that will publish it. The same relationship holds true for other kinds of knowledge in the profession. Consequently, how members of the profession choose to organize and label their knowledge system affects the generation of knowledge, but it also affects the transportation and use of knowledge.

The following discussion will illustrate these and related points by identifying the profession's current approaches to the organization and labeling of knowledge. Three approaches merit our attention, the first two of which are alternative ways to realize the discipline that Henry advocated. One is *interdisciplinary*, and it provides for the organization and labeling of knowledge about traditional disciplines such as psychology, sociology, and physiology. As in the case of psychology of sport cited above, knowledge bears the name of the parent discipline and is organized as a part of it; for this reason psychology of sport and its counterparts are called *subdisciplines*.

A second approach is *crossdisciplinary*. As the descriptor suggests, knowledge is organized and labeled in this approach without any affiliation with a single discipline such as psychology. Rather, inquiry proceeds across disciplinary boundaries, resulting in a new combination of knowledge that stems from parts of psychology, sociology, history, and so on. The common denominator for such diverse knowledge allows it to be woven into a usable whole, and physical and ludic activities and the questions surrounding them are this common denominator. Thus, whereas an interdisciplinary framework is discipline-driven, a crossdisciplinary framework is question-driven. Investigators must cross many disciplines in order to generate and organize their knowledge in relation to their questions. This knowledge bears labels such as "motor control" and "sport studies," which are not tied to any one discipline but instead suggest that knowledge is integrated around a common set of questions and concerns about physical and ludic activities.

A third approach to the organization and labeling of knowledge is rooted in the disciplinary movement and in the history of the profession. This approach is tied to teaching physical education, predicated upon the assumption that the missions and subject matter of physical education are tied to school programs. Therefore, knowledge is organized around the related tasks of teacher-coaches and is called physical education, or a modern counterpart such as *sport pedagogy.*

These three approaches now compete for the favor of the profession's members. Each can be better understood in relation to the disciplinary movement that Henry launched, and each merits analysis in relation to the knowledge system and the kind of future it will allow for the profession. Let's begin with the interdisciplinary framework and its subdisciplines.

The Subdisciplines

The disciplinary movement, as discussed initially in chapter 3, caused change and controversy in many parts of the profession. The profession's knowledge system was affected most, particularly its mechanisms for generating and organizing knowledge. You may recall that Franklin Henry advocated a crossdisciplinary framework. What resulted initially, however, was an interdisciplinary framework from which a number of "subdisciplines" emerged. Even today these subdisciplines represent a way to organize and label some of the profession's knowledge. Identifying these subdisciplines will illustrate how the organization and labeling of knowledge affects its generation, why the disciplinary movement has been a divisive force in the profession and, as a result, what the potential differences are between an interdisciplinary and a crossdisciplinary framework.

The emergence of the subdisciplines is readily understandable, considering historic circumstances. When Henry called for an academic discipline in 1964, there were only a few disciplinarians on physical education faculties. How, then, could scientists and scholars be educated and trained to develop this discipline? Clearly, prospective investigators in the early 1960s could not secure the proper preparation in most physical education departments.

Therefore, many of today's faculty marched off to disciplines such as physiology, engineering, psychology, sociology, history, and philosophy to prepare for the dual role of teacher and scholar. The fruits of their learning in these traditional disciplines were then brought back to departments of physical education and kinesiology. From special terminologies to basic concepts to research methodologies, these faculty members borrowed substance from the traditional disciplines.

They viewed their work as a subset of these traditional disciplines; for example, the sociology of sport was part of sociology, the physiology of exercise was part of physiology, and so on. Many called themselves sociologists and physiologists, not physical educators, for they were working in a subdiscipline for physical education. They formed in one department a group of specialists, each of whom was identified with a traditional discipline. The organizational framework they embraced in the process was interdisciplinary. It brought together a diverse group of specialists whose only common bond was a fascination with studying human involvement in physical and ludic activities.

Before examining some of the consequences of this interdisciplinary framework, it is appropriate to identify and describe briefly the subdisciplines. You should note that in virtually every instance the label for the subdiscipline includes the name of the appropriate parent discipline. This is a central feature of an interdisciplinary framework.

In principle, any discipline offering insight into physical and ludic activities can potentially be called a subdiscipline. Six of these are among the best developed and are commonly labeled as:

Physiology of exercise
Biomechanics of sport
Sociology of sport
History of sport
Philosophy of sport
Psychology of sport and physical activity

Let's take a closer look at each subdiscipline.

The Physiology of Exercise

The physiology of exercise, more commonly called exercise physiology, has enjoyed an enduring tradition in the field. According to David Lamb (1972), the exercise physiologist's academic task is,

> to describe the changes that occur in organ and organismic function as a result of single (acute) or repeated (chronic) doses of exercise and to explain how those functional changes occur. (pp. 16-17)

Scientific inquiry prevails in exercise physiology with most of the research conducted in laboratories. Special facilities are necessary because the research requires specialized, sophisticated, and expensive equipment that usually is not portable. Often the environmental conditions (e.g., temperature, relative humidity) must also be controlled. Also, researchers in exercise physiology use both humans and animals as subjects.

Animals are used for studying responses to exercise at the neurophysiological and biochemical levels. Humans are used whenever possible, however, because it is their physiological responses that must be understood. Of interest to exercise physiologists are responses to exercise such as changes in muscle size and composition, changes in heart rate and size, changes in blood flow and composition, and changes in body composition.

Biomechanics of Sport

Biomechanicians are interested in the coordinated actions of muscles and bones in producing movement. Especially significant to them is the relationship between the body's structure and its function in physical and ludic activities. For years this area of study in physical education was called kinesiology with the term biomechanics of sport introduced only recently. With this new term, moreover, has come an expanded range of interest.

In addition to the more traditional emphasis on body structure and function, biomechanicians analyze sport performance and equipment. They seek to understand the components of efficient or maximal performance from an applied physics perspective. In order to accomplish this task, biomechanicians conduct studies in the field, in the laboratory, and by means of films and computerized simulations.

The Sociology of Sport

Sociology of sport, or sport sociology, borrows its terminology, concepts, and methodology from the well established discipline of sociology. In fact, sport sociology is a formal subdiscipline of sociology and is listed as such in North American sociological associations. Sport clearly is the focus, although all ludic activities (e.g., play, games) that form part of sport's evolution are included in the subject matter.

The sociologist is primarily interested in social phenomena (Loy, 1972). The emphasis here is on the collective social products, such as sport, of people and their societies. These social phenomena can be distinguished from characteristics and behaviors of selected individuals, for studying the individual is the psychologist's goal. By contrast, sociologists examine the enduring patterns of social organization found in a society and then attribute meanings and functions to them. Sport is one such pattern, existing apart from the whims of selected individuals and having identifiable meanings and functions in North America. Therefore, it is open and appropriate to sociological inquiry.

The two primary forms of sociological inquiry are classical and quantitative study. Classical sociology is a form of scholarly inquiry, rooted in history and often equated with history. In contrast, quantitative sociology attempts to understand sport through scientific methods such as surveys and observation.

Even though these two forms of study differ, the questions asked by the sociologist stem from the same discipline. For example, inquiry may be directed toward the functions of sport in producing social control and change, the content of what people learn through participation in sport, sport's contributions to the prevention of delinquency, or managerial styles and functions in sport organization.

The History of Sport

Sport history, like sport sociology, is a rather new field. There has been an enduring interest in the history of physical education, but this differs from the history of sport. We studied physical education's history in chapter 2 in order to provide newcomers to the field with a family tree of important legacies from the profession. By contrast, the history of sport is more comprehensive and dispassionate. Its focus includes the roles of physical educators and their programs in popularizing sport and sporting heritage in all facets of society.

Sport history usually is chronological or social. Chronology in sport probably is most familiar, written in the language of high school history texts. Important dates, places, and actors are listed in order, together describing what happened in a certain time and place. If the history gives an explanation of events, it usually is sketchy at best.

Social history embellishes description with explanation. Instead of seeking a chronology in the strictest sense, social historians direct their efforts toward intriguing trends, themes, and behavior patterns in sport such as professionalism, commercialism, and crowd control. They attend to the ways sport has been influenced in the past by societal forces and actors, and vice versa. A social history that emphasizes explanation is somewhat like classical inquiry in sport sociology, differing only in terminology and concepts.

Myriad questions interest sport historians. When did the informal games of urban dwellers become transformed into modern sport? Why? What roles did the mass media, technology, industry, and the cities play in the rise of sport? In what other periods of history did significant forms of ludic behavior exist, and how were these forms shaped by conditions of the times? Sport historians are writing an increasing array of descriptive-chronological and social histories to answer such questions.

The Philosophy of Sport

Sport philosophy grew in part from the traditional interest in physical education for history, philosophy, and principles. Indeed, such courses have always been part of undergraduate major programs with special textbooks for each. Philosophies of physical education, however, deal with educational thought and its relationship to the design and delivery of school physical education programs, whereas sport philosophy follows sport exclusively.

The province of all philosophers, including those in sport, has eroded over the years. At one time in the development of formal knowledge there was but one discipline—theology, the "Queen of Sciences." Later, as supernatural or religious explanations for everyday occurrences no longer satisfied people, another discipline evolved—philosophy, which meant a love of wisdom. Then, with the advent of science, more and more disciplines emerged in response to special questions requiring equally special methodologies. The once all-encompassing philosophy was gradually redefined in the process, so that the history, philosophy, and principles of physical education became sport history, sport sociology, and sport psychology. The domain of philosophy had thus become smaller. Yet philosophy has survived to seek answers to many unique questions.

Sport philosophers address questions of meaning. Where the use or abuse of language has obscured meaning, their task is to give order and clarity to the written and spoken word, as well as to explore the significance of nonverbal communication. In addition, sport philosophers strive to uncover the meaning and significance of human involvement in ludic activities. Here personal reactions to the activity are linked to larger questions regarding human existence and order in the universe.

Philosophers also entertain questions of what is and is not knowledge. They direct their efforts to the foundational level, seeking to discover what rules and criteria people use when they claim to possess knowledge. For example, when people say they know volleyball, what do they mean? What criteria are they using? Do they know *about* volleyball, *how to play* volleyball, or both?

Finally, philosophers examine behavior in sport. Depending on their pet interests, they may ask if the behavior is beautiful and serves as an art form, if the behaviors are right or proper, or if what they observe is good or bad. In other words, sport philosophers are interested in questions of aesthetics, ethics, and morals. Like other questions in sport philosophy, these often are spawned by the parent discipline.

The Psychology of Sport

The psychology of sport (and physical activity) is the sixth subdiscipline. As suggested earlier, the psychologist examines characteristics and behaviors of individuals. Although the parent discipline of psychology has many competing schools of thought, each with its own investigative method, science has dominated this subdiscipline. Furthermore, at least three areas of specialization have emerged in it—growth and motor development, motor learning and performance, and sport psychology.

The earliest programs in teacher education included growth and motor development, and this subject remains viable. However, the content has expanded over the past two decades to include all relevant aspects of child development. The focus now is on relationships between involvement in physical and ludic activities and this larger question of child development. In other words, specialists in this area are interested both in biology (as in the growth of bones and muscles) and behavior (as in how exercise affects the child's overall development).

Specialists in motor learning and performance study conditions that facilitate versus those that reduce the ability to learn and perform in physical and ludic activities. They employ a range of equipment and experimental tasks. For example, research in this area may include a person's ability to press a lever or button on cue. These researchers entertain questions such as: How do people process new information and skills? How does previous instruction in tennis affect persons wishing to learn badminton? How does anxiety influence performance, and how does performance in various situations induce anxiety?

For their part, psychologists examine the attitudes, attributes, and personalities of athletes in particular, with a more general focus on persons involved in physical and ludic activities. How does competition affect young children? Do athletes differ from nonathletes? Are persons of certain personality types drawn to sport, or does sport help produce persons with a certain type of personality? In order to research these questions, psychologists, like sociologists, employ surveys or questionnaires as well as observational techniques. And although sport psychology is still new, it is growing very rapidly. Combined with the areas of growth and motor development and motor learning and performance, it rates with exercise physiology in constituting one of the best developed subdisciplines.

Limitations of the Interdisciplinary Framework

We have sketched the subject matter of each of the subdisciplines and provided a small sample of questions that investigators address. Though intriguing, these questions are not unique to an interdisciplinary framework. All can be accommodated in a crossdisciplinary approach. The issue, then, is whether the interdisciplinary framework is the best way to generate, organize, and label knowledge for the profession. It probably is not, yet this conclusion must be prefaced by recognizing its uses.

The interdisciplinary framework has been useful for at least two reasons. It allowed the disciplinary foundation Henry advocated to get off the ground, and it brought back into the profession scholars who were adequately prepared to do research and to train and educate the scholars of the future. Adequate testimony to these contributions exists in the wealth of literature and the number of graduate programs now characterizing physical education.

Yet the interdisciplinary approach has five serious limitations. First, the study of physical and ludic activities in this framework is a means to another end instead of being an end in its own right. The intent in an interdisciplinary framework is to use sport, for example, to further develop the parent discipline. This invites a number of unfortunate consequences. It means a unidimensional view — that of the parent discipline — is given to physical and ludic activities. Thus, although human involvement in activities is multidimensional, only a single, selective view of it is possible in a subdiscipline.

A second set of limitations is that the separate identities of faculty (e.g., I am a sport psychologist) and their course (e.g., this is sport psychology) undercut any claims to uniqueness by a department of kinesiology or physical education. Clearly, these faculty members and their courses could be housed just as easily, if not better, in the parent disciplines because so much of the substance in these courses is borrowed from the parent discipline. If the courses from the six subdisciplines and the faculty offering them were located in the parent discipline, students would not have to learn six different terminologies. As it stands, however, students must learn the jargon from the parent discipline *before* they can gain an understanding of physical and ludic activities. Aside from the ways this may interfere with learning, it also delays work toward a common, unique terminology for physical and ludic activities. (Examples of such a terminology already appear in Great Britain and West Germany.)

In addition, this interdisciplinary framework often requires completing a host of prerequisites in parent disciplines before beginning subdisciplinary study in physical education. This means that the latter study frequently is postponed until the third and fourth years in the major, which affects graduate programs. Since graduate programs begin where undergraduate programs end, greater content and sophistication in graduate study cannot occur until undergraduates are able to learn more about physical and ludic activities in the first two years in the major. But the interdisciplinary framework prevents this.

The interdisciplinary approach also is limited in that it severs personal performance experiences from performance analysis, even though the two are strongly related. There really is no need for performance courses and experiences in an interdisciplinary framework because the focus is strictly on the parent discipline and how it can be developed using physical and ludic activities. Whether the student has any skill or experience in these activities is irrelevant. It neglects the student who wishes to work in a profession combining performance and performance analysis. In other words, the primary goal in an interdisciplinary framework is knowledge about performance as it applies to the parent discipline.

A fourth limitation is revealed in the relationship between the generation, organization, and labeling of knowledge and its use. When knowledge is packaged in such specialized subdisciplines, its applicability to the real world often is concealed and reduced. This happens because the results of inquiry are published in journals for the parent discipline, making them difficult for most professionals to retrieve. The language is unfamiliar and the studies themselves are quite specialized. This also holds true for the organization and conduct of courses in the undergraduate major. The point is, even if individuals can understand and retrieve this knowledge, they still face the task of blending it together for use in their work. It is like trying to assemble the pieces of a complex puzzle without a picture of how the puzzle should look! Thus, the interdisciplinary framework retards the use of knowledge in practice, a serious limitation in any profession.

Finally, the interdisciplinary framework is limited in its effects on social relations among the profession's members. Despite their presence and support in physical education departments, some disciplinarians refuse to think of themselves as part of physical education. Furthermore, some of them feel they have more in common with colleagues in the parent disciplines and many are unsympathetic and disinterested in the professional aspirations of undergraduate students in physical education. This has caused faculty and students in physical education to harbor resentment and distrust, reactions which though understandable are nevertheless divisive.

Thus, significant consequences for the profession result from this interdisciplinary approach to organizing and labeling knowledge. It would appear that long-term consequences outweigh any short-term gains. To reiterate, the issue is not so much whether each subdiscipline's questions are appropriate, but rather, which framework is better for disciplinary inquiry and study. For this reason, a crossdisciplinary framework becomes a more suitable substitute.

A Crossdisciplinary Framework

Henry first called for a crossdisciplinary framework in 1964 and then reissued the call in 1978 with a better explanation of what crossdisciplinary study entails. Other accounts of a crossdisciplinary approach have appeared in the literature (Lawson & Morford, 1979; Morford, Lawson, & Hutton, 1981).

The crossdisciplinary framework was designed to fit phenomena such as physical and ludic activities. The fundamental assumption for such a framework is that only through the combined perspective of several related disciplines can these activities be fully understood. This allows the boundaries of parent disciplines to collapse so that new terms, concepts, and methodologies from the combination of several related subjects may emerge.

In other words, the subdisciplines borrow their questions, terms, and methodologies from the parent disciplines. Inquiry into human involvement in physical and ludic activities thus is *discipline-driven* because, from start to finish, the parent discipline determines how knowledge is generated, organized, and labeled.

The crossdisciplinary approach departs such discipline-driven inquiry. It is *question-driven*; investigators begin with important questions about human involvement in physical and ludic activities and pursue answers across traditional disciplinary boundaries. The resultant knowledge is crossdisciplinary because investigators had to develop portions of several related disciplines in order to acquire it.

The accompanying formula is relatively straightforward: Develop those portions of related disciplines that shed light upon physical and ludic activities. Combine these related areas of the disciplines and integrate them for a multidimensional examination of physical and ludic activities. Assemble the findings within the same framework and then label and describe them accordingly. What results from this formula is a unique frame or discipline for kinesiology and a unique subject matter. This formula is at the heart of a crossdisciplinary framework, for it unifies and gives rise to wholes where the interdisciplinary framework divides and produces specialized parts. It accords importance to personal performance experiences that are wedded to scientific and scholarly analysis (Morford, Lawson, & Hutton, 1981).

In the interdisciplinary framework the labels for knowledge are derived from the parent disciplines, but in the crossdisciplinary approach the labels are unique. Instead of six subdisciplines, the crossdisciplinary approach has two related clusters of knowledge, the first called sport studies and the other called motor control.

The first cluster consists of the related disciplines in social-behavioral sciences and humanities. It combines parts of sociology, history, psychology, philosophy, and anthropology, and may be called sport studies or sociocultural studies of physical and ludic activities. Here play, games, contests, dance, and sport are studied with the assumption that the interplay among individuals, groups, organizations, and society connected with such activities can only be fully understood by clustering these related disciplines. For example, suppose professionals want to know about the popularity of football and basketball in our society. Must they know something about society's influences on these activities? Certainly, and this comes from sociology. Must they have an idea about the influences of culture and subculture on these activities? Yes, and this is drawn from anthropology. Must they understand how individuals are attracted to, and how their development is affected by, these activities? Without a doubt, and this comes from psychology. Is it prerequisite to know why some people see these activities as right or wrong, good or bad? Again, the answer is yes, and this means appropriate portions of philosophy must be developed.

The fruits of crossdisciplinary inquiry appear in the *combination* or blending of perspectives. *Integration* is the rule of thumb for starting investigations, presenting the findings, and organizing coursework. Integration results from question-driven inquiry, and the questions asked also serve as the themes around which knowledge is organized.

The subject matter of sport studies was introduced earlier but it merits another look here:

The socio-historical and contemporary roles of physical and ludic activities in culture, in both primitive and advanced societies, and the contribution of these activities to the emotional, social, physical, and aesthetic development of the individual. (Morford, Lawson, & Hutton, 1981; p. 64)

Scholars who work in sport studies have received some education and training in one or more of these disciplines, yet they are not sport sociologists or sport psychologists. Rather, they are specialists in sport studies who speak the same language, use the same concepts, and share many of the the same methodologies in their inquiry. The questions they entertain are similar to those in some of the related subdisciplines; examples appear in Table 4.

The other cluster of knowledge in kinesiology includes exercise physiology, biomechanics, biochemistry, and portions of psychology. It can be called *motor control*. Here too, relevant parts of these related disciplines are combined and integrated to yield an understanding of the biological and behavioral processes that affect human learning and performance in physical and ludic activities. Students and scholars must know some physiology, psychology, and mechanics in order to address the important questions about physical and ludic activities, but it is in the integration of their methods and results that a crossdisciplinary framework emerges. The subject matter resulting from this type of inquiry is integrated as,

selected biological, psychological, and mechanical factors which are associated with the individual's growth and motor development, functional status, and abilities to engage in physical and ludic activities. (Morford, Lawson, & Hutton, 1981; pp. 63-64)

Thus, faculty in this area of kinesiology are specialists in motor control. The kinds of questions that concern them appear in Table 5.

The questions in Tables 4 and 5 illustrate a major point: The questions often are the same in both crossdisciplinary and interdisciplinary framework. Again, the issue is one of which way is better for organizing and labeling knowledge, considering how it will be generated and how members of the profession will use it. A crossdisciplinary framework appears to be a better choice because (a) it is question-driven, giving a broader, integrated kind of knowledge; (b) it does not require members of the profession to learn the terminologies and concepts of all related parent

Table 4
Questions in Sport Studies

1. What are the differences and similarities between play, games, contests, dance, and sport? How might the experience of the performer differ in each of these ludic activities, and why?
2. What are the functions of sport in society? Can sport be a mechanism for social change? Has it ever been so?
3. In what ways might participation in dance or sport influence the self-concepts of performers? Would their personalities be altered?
4. What are the effects of participation in interscholastic and intercollegiate athletics on academic achievement? Do college and university athletes complete their degree programs? Why or why not?
5. Is sport a performing art? What features of sport allow such a decision? What sociocultural factors have kept people from thinking about sport as a performing art? Can these be changed?
6. Which is worse in sport, the quitter or the cheater? Why? Is it ever appropriate to "bend" the rules in order to win? Do coaches differ from athletes in this, and why?
7. How do ludic preferences and participatory styles vary within the same cultures? What kinds of variation are found across cultures? How might both kinds of variation be explained?
8. How does an audience affect the learning and performance capabilities of students? Of athletes?
9. What is the relationship between what performers believe they have accomplished and actual assessments of their performance?
10. What kinds of stress accompany athletic performance? Is it good or bad? How might it be managed properly?
11. What causes violence among sport fans? Do the same factors cause violence between athletes? Can they be changed?
12. At what age or stage do people develop clear-cut preferences for participation? What is required to alter them at a later time?
13. What happens to professional athletes when they retire from sport?
14. What is the relationship between preferences for physical and ludic activities and socioeconomic status?
15. Is there such a thing as an alienated athlete? What are the causes?
16. How does the emergence of modern sport relate to industrialization? Is sport itself a form of industry?
17. In what ways have forms of dance changed over the past 200 years?
18. List any questions of interest to you.

---

disciplines; (c) it ushers in the unique discipline Henry advocated; (d) it combines performance experiences with performance analysis; (e) it stands to unite rather than divide members of the profession because of their common interest in human involvement in physical and ludic activities; and (f) the broader, com-

Table 5
Questions in Motor Control

---

1. What does the term "skill" mean? Are mental and motor skills the same?
2. What are the best ways to develop skills in students and athletes?
3. How might motor skills be classified?
4. What is the difference between learning and performance? What is the relationship between them? How are learning and performance influenced by psychological factors such as motivation, attitude, and personality?
5. How do individuals vary in their capacities for learning and performance? What kinds of variation may be expected in the same individual? What kinds may be expected among individuals?
6. What is the difference between growth and maturation? How do these factors affect learning and performance?
7. At what age or developmental stage is it appropriate for boys and girls to engage in contact sports?
8. What are the best ways to train and condition athletes for various sports? Are there outcomes other than improved performance?
9. What kinds of biochemical changes accompany intensive training and conditioning and what is their significance?
10. What are the different types of muscles in the body, and how do they affect performance in specific sports? How are these same muscles affected by performance? Are these effects beneficial or harmful?
11. In what ways may peak performances in sport be simulated on a computer? How may computer simulations be used to improve the performance of athletes?
12. What electrochemical mechanisms enable the brain to send messages to parts of the body during performance? In what ways, if any, may these be improved?
13. How do drugs affect athletic performance and athletes?
14. Are there significant differences in the perceptual abilities of athletes? Can these abilities be altered? Should they be?
15. How does exercise affect bone growth in young children? Can bones be harmed by exercise? If so, when is this likely to happen?
16. What are the roles of the brain and the spinal cord in performance?
17. To what extent are the changes that accompany exercise in animals the same as with humans?
18. List any questions of interest to you.

---

prehensive picture it provides for this involvement enhances the application and use of this knowledge in practice. These advantages double as ways to differentiate this approach from the interdisciplinary one. Together these advantages promise unity at a time when many people are concerned about the future of the profession because of the divisiveness caused by the interdisciplinary approach (e.g., Bressan, 1979).

Nevertheless, there remains a choice between the two approaches as the debate among their advocates continues. Since the choice ultimately will be made by members of the profession, it is everyone's duty to keep informed about both and to act where necessary to persuade others. Yet there is more to learn about the organization of knowledge for the profession, particularly about professional knowledge.

The Organization of Professional Knowledge

In 10 years we may need a separate chapter for discussing professional knowledge. Indeed, inquiry into a number of new careers in physical education is evident now. The fact remains, however, that the most highly developed kind of professional knowledge is that for prospective teacher-coaches in the schools.

Yet even in the case of teacher-coach education, scientific and scholarly inquiry is relatively new. Although some professionals had already suggested the need for such knowledge, it was in 1972 that Lawrence F. Locke offered a penetrating observation to teacher educators in physical education. It is often quoted (cf., Siedentop, 1980, p. 131) and goes like this:

> It continues to be an astonishing fact that the training of physical education teachers has received almost no substantial or systematic attention from professional organizations, journals, and scholars within our field. (Locke, 1972)

This indicates genuine concern over the art and science of teacher education and practice in the schools, with the call for such scholarship rooted in a familiar assumption. That is, the more we learn about teaching physical education, the better the programs and the more effective the teachers can become. For this reason, many teacher educators have proclaimed a discipline of pedagogy for physical education, called sport pedagogy (Haag, 1978). Sport pedagogy is the science of teaching and coaching, and it embraces goals, methods, and evaluative frameworks.

Advocates for such a discipline believe that the generation of knowledge and its application usually are inseparable. Description and explanation are one side of the coin, prescription is the other, and the two sides join to give this discipline an identity. This view of a discipline differs from that provided by Henry. It should therefore come as no surprise that its different assumptions also yield conclusions different from Henry's.

The view of a discipline that combines the generation and application of knowledge is best described by Siedentop (1976; 1980), who argues that although it is always important for investigators in any field to be as neutral and objective as humanly possible, they rarely stop at the stage of generating knowledge. They also apply it in a professional or prescribed way. Thus,

> When exercise physiologists study the relationship between fluid intake during exercise stress and certain physiological parameters, they don't merely report these data and wait for a "professional" to put them in to use. Many state high school athletic associations have made new rules related to the use of full equipment and the availability of water during practices conducted in periods of high heat and humidity. Often, exercise physiologists have been instrumental not only in conducting the research leading to information on which such rules are based, but also in interpreting and disseminating the information so that it affects coaching practices positively. (1980, p. 127)

According to Siedentop, a discipline does not make artificial distinctions between decription and prescription because the two are inevitably intertwined. This assumption underlies a discipline of pedagogy in physical education. In addition, Siedentop and others support sport pedagogy by partly rejecting the discipline Henry proclaimed. While granting some applicability of Henry's disciplinary knowledge, Siedentop speaks for others in citing some reservations:

> Some knowledge developed within the domain of the discipline is totally irrelevant to teaching physical education in the schools and will remain so indefinitely simply because the variables under scrutiny are so molecular that manipulations of tightly-controlled independent variables produce variations that, while of interest to theory, will never be of practical import for the responsible execution of professional skills in school programs of physical education. (1980, p. 130)

Many terms in this quotation are used by researchers and may be unfamiliar, but the point Siedentop makes stands apart from the language. He is saying that much of the disciplinary knowledge does not apply to the teaching of physical education in the schools. That is, he has assumed that kinesiology does not satisfy all of the requirements for prospective teachers, and he is not alone in accepting this assumption. As a consequence, he and others have called for a separate discipline of pedagogy in physical education, based upon three related assumptions.

First, the primary subject matter of physical education is sport, games, dance, and exercise. Second, the primary function of the physical educator has been to teach this subject matter to students. Third, the primary context within which the teaching of this subject matter has been pursued is in schools as part of the general content that citizens of this nation feel is worthwhile to pass on to the next generation. (Siedentop, 1980, p. 128)

Consistent with the line of reasoning we have advanced in previous chapters, Siedentop adds "If you do not accept one or more of these assumptions, then the argument presented [here] will probably not satisfy you" (Siedentop, 1980, p. 128).

To summarize, the discipline of pedagogy in physical education answers the calls for better research and better practice for school physical education programs. The target is increased effectiveness for members of the teaching profession. Underneath all this is a concern for professional standards. Once members of the profession have mastered the specialized knowledge structured within the discipline of pedagogy, they can elevate practice in the schools. The disciplinary structure for pedagogy is thus centered on and limited to schools, and is labeled physical education. The subject matter for this discipline follows suit, for it includes the current substance of these programs—exercise, sport, games, dance, etc.—as well as the teachers and students who participate. Areas of inquiry for pedagogy include teacher characteristics and behavior, student characteristics and behavior, and the interactions of teachers and students within the broad context of the school and the specific context of physical education programs.

Thus, research in the discipline of pedagogy is presumed to bring about improvements in practice. Examples of the kinds of research or the kinds of questions addressed within this disciplinary framework are listed in Table 6.

Table 6
Questions in Sport Pedagogy

---

1. What is the best age or developmental stage to begin learning tennis, golf, and other physical and ludic activities?
2. What is the best way to sequence instruction in activities? What is the best way to group students?
3. What skills do effective teachers possess? What behaviors do effective teachers display? What is the relationship between a teacher's skills or competencies, the teacher's actual behavior, and what students learn?
4. What social and political factors have shaped the design and conduct of school physical education programs?
5. What are the alternative models for teaching and learning, as well as for program structure? What practical results are gained from each?
6. What are the characteristics of incoming physical education majors? How do these characteristics change over 4 years? What happens to these same people when they begin teaching? Are they different after the first year? After 5 years?
7. Do some people drop out of teaching? Is it because they want a change of occupations or because they get "burned-out," working so hard and long that they quit to get a rest?
8. What causes discipline problems among students? What characterizes good programs and teaching that prevent discipline problems?
9. Do students learn more than the formal curriculum in physical education? Does physical education have a "hidden curriculum" wherein students learn obedience to authorities? What are the functions of school physical education with regard to social control and social change?
10. What models and strategies are most appropriate for introducing change in physical education? Which ones work under what circumstances? Which ones have failed in the past?
11. What kinds of questions about school physical education do students like you bring to an undergraduate major program? Are you willing to list them?

This discussion of the pedagogy discipline is best concluded by inquiring about its future. From the perspective of its advocates, pedagogy merits separate and equal time compared to kinesiology, where equal applies to resources as much as to claims on one's time during undergraduate education. Separation from kinesiology follows logically from the assumption about that discipline's inapplicability to teaching physical education in the schools. One aim, then, is a kind of peaceful coexistence in the same department, usually under the label "physical education."

Siedentop points to another alternative, however, involving the gradual evolution of kinesiology and the discipline of pedagogy in physical education into two separate departments (Siedentop, 1980, p. 119). This proposal is best understood with reference to an earlier point: The subdisciplines and their proponents have been a divisive force in physical education! Ironically, Siedentop's personal proposal is equally divisive in one sense, yet in another it simply reflects a different viewpoint of the subject matter and missions for physical education than that presented in chapter 5.

Having recognized the intensity of personal beliefs about the organization and labeling of knowledge, it is appropriate to return to that knowledge called sport pedagogy, or pedagogy in physical education. Considering the definitions introduced by its advocates, it is possible to call this disciplinary knowledge; but considering the definitions provided here and in previous chapters, it is professional knowledge. It is to be used by teacher-coaches to prescribe for students and athletes. Both concerns, essentially the same, represent a call for more and better scientific and scholarly inquiry into this facet of work in the profession, with that call being answered at an ever-increasing rate.

Returning now to the questions in Table 6, would answers to those questions be of interest and use only to teacher-coaches in schools? Probably not, since the knowledge resulting from those answers appears useful for professionals outside the schools. This, then, is the crucial issue about the organization and labeling of knowledge, including who will generate it. How can it be organized and labeled to insure maximal coverage and use? This question is what makes the label "sport pedagogy" so appealing (Haag, 1978). That term is already used in Europe to include a broad range of knowledge about the roles of teachers, instructors, and coaches in various agencies, and it appears that this term may gain similar popularity in North America.

Three related questions remain, however. Does this professional knowledge stand by itself for the profession, or does it serve to complement the disciplinary knowledge proclaimed by Henry? Should the profession's missions and subject matter be limited to school programs? Is the applicability of disciplinary subject matter to school as limited as Siedentop and others suggest? Some advocates of sport pedagogy might suggest that this knowledge should stand by itself because disciplinary knowledge is of little help in school programs; hence, the missions and subject matter of the profession should be tied to school programs. This point of view deserves to be voiced and understood, but so do others.

Previous chapters have underlined such a different point of view, one revealed partly in competing answers to the same three questions. It was argued in those chapters that professional knowledge complements disciplinary knowledge, and chapters 5 through 7 cited examples of the ways in which both kinds of knowledge help to improve career preparation and work performance. Chapters 5 and 6 discussed how the missions of the profession already have expanded to include careers other than teaching/coaching, in agencies other than schools. Chapter 7 also discussed how disciplinary knowledge is now included in many elementary and secondary school physical education curricula. What better indication could one find of the application of disciplinary knowledge to school programs than the current practice of teaching students the knowledge that was formerly restricted to physical education majors? Another question should be added: Who really knows what school programs will look like in 30 years, or whether they will continue to exist? Surely this debatable question suggests that it is risky to limit the profession to school programs of today.

Thus we conclude that pedagogical inquiry, although important, is just a part of the profession's concern, not the whole. To limit the profession to it alone is like telling an automobile driver to focus exclusively on the rear view mirror. That is, this restricted view of the profession represents its past, not its future. Although this would provide some sense of where we've been, we must also map where we are in relation to the future we wish to create. Pedagogical inquiry will produce knowledge that will help us create the future, whether in schools or elsewhere, but the fact remains that even today it is no longer possible to limit the profession's operations to schools. New recruits, others in the profession, and society itself simply will not be satisfied with anything less than the growing, diversified profession to which you are invited.

Summary

The organization and labeling of knowledge forms an important part of the knowledge system for physical education, as it affects the generation of knowledge as well as its subsequent use in practice. Before long, the profession's members will have to choose between competing frameworks and labels for the organization of knowledge in physical education. They can make a reasoned choice only by understanding the operations of the profession's knowledge system and its relationship to the competing alternatives.

Although Henry spoke from a crossdisciplinary framework, an interdisciplinary framework also emerged. Many of the questions investigators choose to pursue are the same in both frameworks, but the similarities end there. Inquiry in the subdisciplines is discipline-driven, whereas a question-driven approach requires the investigator to cross over several related disciplines. And the differences only begin here, while more are revealed in the way knowledge is packaged, labeled, stored, sequenced, and used. When the needs and interests of the profession are considered, a crossdisciplinary framework is suggested as a superior choice.

Scientific and scholarly inquiry into the work roles in physical education is relatively new. The body of professional knowledge about teaching and coaching is the most developed and may be called sport pedagogy; the broad organization of this knowledge allows it to include and serve professionals outside as well as inside the schools. Whether this knowledge stands by itself or complements disciplinary knowledge remains a topic of debate in the profession. Debates should not, however, blur the importance of this knowledge.

Clearly, the organization and labeling of the profession's knowledge are influenced directly by members' views of the subject matter and missions for physical education. Debate, controversy, and even confusion are thus to be expected in this part of the field's knowledge system because physical education is a profession in transition and its knowledge system reflects this fact. The challenge is to find ways of organizing and labeling the results of inquiry, ways that accommodate the breadth, depth, richness, uniqueness, and utility of the profession's knowledge.

Supplementary Activities

Self-testing Exercise

After reading chapter 8 and reviewing its contents, you should be able to:

1. Identify the importance of the organization of knowledge, citing its relationship to the generation and use of knowledge in the profession;
2. Explain the need and the rationale for the study of sport pedagogy in physical education;
3. Identify the characteristics, components, and limitations of an interdisciplinary framework for kinesiology;
4. Identify the characteristics, components, and advantages of a crossdisciplinary framework for kinesiology;
5. Distinguish between the three frameworks for organizing knowledge;
6. Choose between the competing alternatives and be prepared to justify your choice.

Class Activities

1. Find as many journals as you can which contain scientific, scholarly, and experiential knowledge. Pool the results in class. How many different journals are there? Which ones seem best suited for work roles? Why? What descriptors are the best indicators of such knowledge?
2. Interview other faculty members for their views on sport pedagogy and their choice on an inter- or cross-disciplinary framework? How are their views colored by their interests and responsibilities? Do they think that questions such as these are important?

Questions for Discussion

1. Should teacher education be separated from disciplinary inquiry and disciplinarians? Why, or why not?
2. Should members of the profession try to reach a consensus on the organization and labeling of its knowledge. Why, or why not?
3. Does the disciplinary subject matter kinesiology have any use in your intended career? Explain.
4. In your chosen career, how might you find, read, and then use new knowledge as it is produced?
5. Should courses in the sociology of sport, psychology of sport, physiology of exercise, and the like be offered in physical education, or in the respective, parent disciplines? Why, or why not?

Sources for Additional Reading

BRESSAN, E. 2001: The profession is dead—Was it murder or suicide? *Quest*, 1979, **31**(1), 77-82.

BROEKHOFF, J. Physical education as a profession. *Quest*, 1979, **31**(2), 244-254.

HENRY, F.M. The academic discipline of physical education. *Quest*, 1978, **29**, 13-29.

LOCKE, L.F. Introduction. *Quest*, 1972, **18**.

MORFORD, W.R. Toward a profession, not a craft. *Quest*, 1972, **18**, 88-93.

SIEDENTOP, D. On tilting at treadmills while Rome burns. *Quest*, 1972, **18**, 94-97.

CHAPTER 9
The transportation and communication of knowledge

Preceding chapters have discussed how knowledge in physical education is generated and organized, and this one will look at ways of transporting this knowledge to the members. If new knowledge is to be useful, it must be transported, in communicable form, from the place it was generated and organized to the people who should use it. This step is crucial in any profession, particularly in physical education with its range of career opportunities. After all, if potential users do not learn of new knowledge, do not receive it or cannot understand it, there is little hope it will be used to improve, justify, or change practice.

As we analyze the transportation and communication of knowledge in physical education, we will identify the related issues, problems, and approaches. It should become clear that future improvements are necessary in this part of the knowledge system, but this does not deny that valuable approaches already exist. Rather, we would call for formal, systematic attention to what has and has not happened in this part of the knowledge system with a look at some of the reasons. Perhaps when new members of the profession understand the process as it exists today, they can chart an altered course into the future in which new knowledge has a greater chance of being used because it is received and understood by intended users.

Conflicting Views of Practitioners

First we need to consider the teachers, coaches, managers, planners, and others in physical education because they are the primary (although not the only) persons who will use new knowledge. Various members of the profession view these practitioners in conflicting ways, a significant finding because conflicting views lead to entirely different approaches for transporting and communicating knowledge. We will examine them by presenting many of the most pressing issues for this part of the knowledge system in physical education.

Autonomous or Dependent Practitioners?

Should practitioners use new knowledge in practice? From the very beginning, this book has argued that such use of knowledge is a distinguishing feature of professional work. New knowledge should always be used in appropriate circumstances to improve, justify, and change practice.

But are practitioners independently able to use the latest results from inquiry? Members hold conflicting views on this, based on the role of professional education and the long-term demands of practice.

It is unrealistic to expect practitioners to carry out responsibilities for which they have not been adequately educated and trained. This is especially true when the task involves working with the results from increasingly sophisticated inquiry. If the independent use of knowledge is desirable, then professional education programs in our field will have to spend more time teaching students how to use the results of inquiry in practice.

When we understand that physical education is a profession in transition and that its emphasis on the generation and organization of knowledge is rather recent, we have every reason to anticipate a difference between the practitioners of yesterday and those of tomorrow. Practitioners who received their professional education and training before the middle 1960s may not be able to appreciate and use the results of inquiry. Tomorrow's practitioners—the introductory students of today—are in a position to gain the prerequisite education and training.

In other words, one's answer to this question depends largely on his or her perspective of the profession. When past organization, content, and conduct of professional education programs are identified, it is possible to argue that practitioners cannot use results from inquiry in their work. On the other hand, when considering today's professional education, one would argue that practitioners *should* be able to use knowledge as it is produced.

Professional education, however, is just one side to consider as the demands of practice in physical education also may influence the practitioner's use of research. Again one could argue that the way practice is performed now and the way that it should be performed in the future are different, and a clear relationship exists between professional education and practice in this regard: New forms of professional education may usher in new forms of practice. However, this future possibility does not erase the present demands on practitioners. For example, many may not see the *relevance* of new knowledge in practice. They may not have the *time* to read these results nor the *ability* to do so, given the special language of the publications. Furthermore, perhaps few *rewards* accompany the use of knowledge. Such conditions can influence any answer to a question about the abilities of practitioners to use new knowledge in practice. Members who answer "yes" assume that today's newer form of professional education will automatically change conditions in practice, whereas others see these conditions as unchanging and answer the question with a resounding "no." Even if new practitioners are prepared in higher education, they argue, after working for 10 years they will have lost the interest and ability to stay abreast *independently* of new knowledge as it is produced.

Here, then, are conflicting views that influence the entire knowledge system for physical education, especially its mechanisms for transporting and communicating knowledge. Those who answer "yes" may not worry much about the transportation of knowledge and may show less concern for its communication; they have assumed that new forms of professional education will prepare practitioners for using knowledge and allow them to change practice as well. In contrast, those who answer "no" are dissatisfied with the contributions of professional education. They will devote time, effort, and resources to help practitioners use new knowledge, beginning with the way it is transported and communicated.

Should Practitioners Generate Knowledge?

Conflicting views of practitioners in this light also trigger different approaches to the transportation and communication of knowledge. Some persons in the profession would answer "no" to the above question, suggesting that practitioners have not received the education and training necessary to generate knowledge and that the demands of practice will not allow it. But this rationale may not tell the whole story.

Persons answering in the negative often are scholars and scientists with strong views about which kinds of inquiry and knowledge are superior. Their own education and training, together with their work in generating knowledge, have helped color their views. They believe scientific and scholarly knowledge attained through structured forms of inquiry are always superior to experiential knowledge gained by reflective inquiry. In fact, some scholars and scientists may not even be willing to accept the notion that experiential knowledge deserves the status of "knowledge."

Without deciding whether such views are appropriate, let's see how they determine approaches to transporting and communicating knowledge. Researchers usually see the problem as one of *applying* knowledge to practice. Metaphorically, they often construct a one-way street from scientists and scholars to practitioners, thereby restricting a mutual flow of knowledge. In addition, these persons may believe that special communication of knowledge is necessary because they assume that practitioners are unable to retrieve this material independently. The titles of their works reveal this bias, often appearing as "What Research Tells the Practitioner about (Volleyball, Physical Fitness, etc.)," or simply "Research for the Practitioner."

The attempt to apply is commendable in its own right, and it is part of a knowledge system for physical education and other professions. But such a process also includes some hidden assumptions about practitioners and practice. In fact, a more accurate title of the publications might read "What *Researchers* Tell the Practitioner about . . ."! That is, scientists and scholars who generated the knowledge also wrote the reports; they are communicating the research. Among their assumptions are: Scientists and scholars have the task of finding the best way for practitioners to accomplish work; only scientists and scholars can supply the knowledge that answers all of the practitioner's needs; scientific and scholarly knowledge is superior to experiential knowledge; thus, knowledge must go in one directon—from those who know (scientists and scholars) to those needing to know (practitioners), and therefore the task is one of *applying* knowledge to practice.

The other side of this argument leads to approaches to transport knowledge. Some members of the profession would point to the role of professional education in preparing practitioners for reflective inquiry, accepting the need for experiential knowledge because they believe scientific and scholarly knowledge will always be incomplete. They would argue that any knowledge *for* practice must stem partly *from* practice and from those performing it. Therefore, they would grant the experiential knowledge gained by practitioners a status equal to scientific and scholarly knowledge. By extension, reflective practitioners would gain equal status with scientists and scholars, the assumption being that scientists and scholars interested in practice can learn from practitioners just as readily as practitioners can learn from them.

Scientists, scholars, and practitioners thus are seen as part of the same team; their roles are different yet complementary, as are the forms of inquiry they use and the kind of knowledge they generate. Of course, scientific and scholarly knowledge should be applied for use in practice, but practice also provides the acid test for whether such knowledge works. Whether it does or does not, practitioners must communicate the results back to the scientists and scholars. In addition, any new findings that practitioners uncover in their work through careful reflection must be communicated to scientists and scholars to help them with their inquiry. Thus, knowledge cannot merely be *applied*, it must be *transported*! Furthermore, even if the application of knowledge requires only a one-way street, its transportation requires a two-way street. The way you choose to deal with this issue will depend on the views you come to accept about practitioners' abilities, their roles, and the kinds of knowledge that must be used in practice.

Models for the Application and Transportation of Knowledge

The business of either applying or transporting knowledge in communicable form confronts all professions. Toward this end, alternative models have been designed and tested, and members of the profession must choose among these models or perhaps design new ones better suited to our needs.

Before describing the competing models in physical education, let's clarify just what we can expect from such a model. Whether you look at toy models for cars and airplanes, or models for the application or transportation of knowledge in a profession, you always find a model *for* something, not *of* it. That is, a model provides some likeness; rarely is it an exact replica. Consequently, the choice among models in a profession involves judgment by its members; they must choose a model that best corresponds to the process and products they endorse. The model helps alert members to important parts of the process that might otherwise have gone unnoticed. Such a model is a means to an end—improved practice—rather than an end in its own right. It serves only to guide practice; it is not a complete picture of it.

Four models for the application and transportation of knowledge merit consideration by all the profession's members. They are called research and development, social interaction, problem-solving, and knowledge-linking (House, 1979), and each will be discussed in relation to the preceding discussion on conflicting views of practitioners.

Research and Development Model

Many corporations have separate divisions called "research and development," and such a model for transporting knowledge was derived largely from this corporate practice. Because a profession must serve its individual members in numerous, often scattered locations, proponents of the research and development model tacked on another label—*diffusion*. The resulting Research, Development, and Diffusion (RD&D) model thus emphasizes knowledge generation and flow (diffusion) to a number of different locations.

A corporation's research and development division has two responsibilities: to improve existing products and invent new ones. Consider, for example, an automobile corporation, where prototypes for new automobiles are developed in laboratories and then road tested to insure quality. Ultimately, when the car has met acceptable standards and appears to be marketable, it is distributed to dealers who sell it to consumers.

In the RD&D model, knowledge is generated and field tested by scientists and occasionally scholars under controlled laboratory conditions. When the knowledge is deemed ready, and often this occurs when it can be organized into a technology, efforts are made to distribute it to potential users. The RD&D model treats knowledge like a product that must be transferred from where it was generated to where it will be used.

This model primarily focuses on the producers of knowledge and their product, giving little attention to the distribution of knowledge or the needs of practitioner-consumers. Four major assumptions underlie this model and evaluating each may help determine whether the model is desirable.

First, it is assumed that knowledge generated under highly controlled conditions in laboratories will apply readily to the practitioner's workplace. Second, the knowledge and technologies so generated are assumed to be applicable to similar agencies (e.g., all schools, all recreation centers), which assumes, in turn, that these agencies and the roles that practitioners fill in them are (and should be) the same. Third, it is assumed that the knowledge should be applied without question because scientific and scholarly knowledge are superior to all other kinds of knowledge since scientists and scholars know more than practitioners. Fourth, it is assumed that knowledge, like a new automobile, requires only appropriate packaging and delivery and that its use will be automatic. These assumptions are not neutral. They incorporate conflicting views of the practitioner and include new issues causing differences of opinion.

On the other hand, the strength of the RD&D model is that it asks members of the profession to find the best way to accomplish work. It aims at increasing practitioners' efficiency by improving their practice and it appears to work well under two conditions: where there is much consensus among practitioners regarding the goals of work and their roles in performing it, and when inquiry gives rise to technologies that do show the best way to perform work. Again this rationale comes from corporate thinking.

However, these two conditions often are not present. For example, physical education teachers in the same school frequently disagree about goals for their programs and their respective work roles. Furthermore, technology in physical education is limited; but even where it is not, research leads us to question whether a technology that works in one school will work in another. Put differently, it is doubtful that there is a single best way to perform work.

Some side effects associated with the RD&D model also emerge as problems preventing the use of knowledge. Among the most deleterious are that the practitioner is treated as a passive adopter of new knowledge and gets no credit for being able to make fundamental decisions about the substance of work or the way it is performed. The practitioner's role in this model is to use the knowledge presented, without question, much like an assembly line worker must obey supervisors. After all, it is assumed that the process of research and development has yielded the best way to accomplish one's responsibilities. But consider the side effects! If practitioners are just passive adopters, then their reflective inquiry and experiential knowledge are not needed. Yet practitioners have valuable experiential knowledge, and if they are told it is inferior they may take offense and avoid sharing it.

Another side effect of the RD&D model is that it views practitioners as second-class citizens in the profession, subordinate to researchers. This impairs social relationships between members of the same profession and sets up a barrier to the transportation and communication of knowledge for practice. It becomes an issue of self-concept and pride, with neither group inclined to accept knowledge from the other. Such side effects, and the four major assumptions for this model, have caused some members of the profession to question its appropriateness; yet others have chosen to endorse it.

Social Interaction Model

The social interaction model takes its strength from a major weakness of the RD&D model. An RD&D model focuses on knowledge and those who supply it, whereas a social interaction model, as its name suggests, emphasizes the relationships that must be built and maintained between researchers and practitioners. These social relationships are intended to bridge communication between the scientists, scholars, and practitioners. The need for easy communication is assumed because these two groups in the profession inhabit two different worlds. This "two communities" view of practitioners versus scientists and scholars apparently is very popular in other professions (Caplan, 1973; Dunn, 1980; Rothman, 1980).

Another contrast in the two models is that the RD&D model is product-oriented, whereas the social interaction model highlights the *process* by which knowledge is transported and communicated. In fact, such an overriding emphasis is placed on the process of transporting knowledge that the knowledge itself is often forced to take a back seat, revealing one of this model's limitations.

Where the RD&D model assumes that knowledge will apply equally to all similar agencies, the social interaction model assumes that each agency is at least somewhat unique, and furthermore, that the meanings and values of the practitioners are unique. Therefore, scientists, scholars, and practitioners all play active roles in establishing relationships to yield an understanding of this uniqueness. In this process, knowledge may flow from those who generate it (scientists and scholars) to the practitioners who should use it.

Thus, the social interaction model did not depart radically from the RD&D model, but in fact emerged after people witnessed the side effects of the RD&D model. The social interaction model therefore was not a revolutionary proposal; it was a hybrid that included key parts of the RD&D model. One must not lose sight of this fact when choosing among alternative models.

Problem-solving Model

The problem-solving model evolved at about the same time as the social interaction model and for the same reason. The RD&D model's limitations caused people to seek alternatives, and like the social interaction model, the problem-solving approach emerged as a hybrid of the RD&D model. Again like the social interaction model, the problem-solving model attends to a weakness in the RD&D approach. The problem-solving model allows practitioners to be active, whereas RD&D assumes they adopt knowledge passively. The RD&D model assumes that scientific and scholarly knowledge or those who produce it are most important to a system for transporting and communicating knowledge; in contrast, the problem-solving model emphasizes the needs, perceptions, and problems of *practitioners*. Hence, it was called a problem-solving model.

The problem-solving model also assumes that active practitioners should control the kind and amount of knowledge transported and communicated. Like the social interaction model, it considers the needs and concerns of practitioners as unique among situations. And like the RD&D and social interaction models, knowledge flows primarily one way; but in this model the practitioners are in control, whereas in the other two, scientists and scholars control the flow of knowledge. This pivotal role for practitioners is a major advantage of the model because it improves the likelihood that the knowledge received will be applied in practice, and because it eliminates some of the side effects of the RD&D model.

However, the weakness in the problem-solving model is that the transportation of knowledge is selective and uneven. Consider that physical education teachers in three different schools may be expected to have different perceptions of needs and problems. As a consequence, the knowledge they seek will vary among schools and perhaps even within the same school. If all outcomes were equal, there would be nothing wrong with this pattern. Yet in the ever increasing instances where knowledge has produced technologies that might be valuable in *all* schools, there is no guarantee these technologies will reach practitioners. Why? Because these teachers may not perceive the need for them. In this sense knowledge is transported selectively. It is uneven because a tremendous flow of knowledge may be directed toward one school while only a trickle goes to another.

The school not receiving such information becomes a stumbling block to the profession, for practitioners not only represent themselves, they also represent one another. Therefore, when unjustified practices exist in one school all teachers in the area are affected, as is the profession at large. So the selective and uneven transportation of knowledge can be viewed as a limitation of the problem-solving model, but the pivotal roles for practitioners can be viewed as one of its strengths.

Linkage Models

The three models presented to this point focus more on one part of the transportation and communication system than others. For example, the RD&D model emphasizes scientists, scholars, and the knowledge *(product)* they produce. The social interaction model promotes the *process* of transporting and communicating knowledge and the social relationships needed. The problem-solving model attends to the role of practitioners in the transportation and communication of knowledge, thus emphasizing the *context* for the system. Linkage models (Havelock, 1969) were designed to feature all these parts of the system as well as some parts not in the other models.

Linkage models begin from the assumption that practitioners, scientists, and scholars are equal partners in the profession, and that the production, organization, transportation, communication, and use of knowledge are interrelated parts of the same system. Like the social interaction model, they emphasize the process of transporting and communicating knowledge; but linkage models direct attention toward establishing permanent bridges, or linkages, between persons in the profession and the organizations in which they work. For example, linkages might exist between a university and a number of local schools, as well as among the schools themselves. These permanent linkages are needed because knowledge must be transported and communicated constantly; it cannot be a one-time affair. And all forms of knowledge, including the experiential, must be transported to all potential users. In some instances (as in linkages between schools) scientists and scholars are not directly involved in the process, although in others they are.

Thus, linkage models grant an active and important role to practitioners as well as to scientists and scholars. Although this rationale is borrowed from the problem-solving model, knowledge still is at center stage in the linkage approach to transportation and communication, and this stems from the RD&D model.

Linkage models have two new features and therefore are not just combinations of the other three models. One feature is the concept of a middle person, a linkage agent who brings together members of the profession inhabiting two different worlds or communities. Persons in this role must understand the demands of practice as well as the requirements and uses of rigorous inquiry. It is assumed that transportation and communication of knowledge require more than permanent relationships; they require people who translate between two different yet complementary kinds of members in the profession—practitioners, and scientists and scholars.

Persons performing these knowledge-linking functions may be faculty members in colleges and universities, district supervisors for physical education, or departmental heads in physical education. Linkage agents often require advanced, specialized forms of education and training because the roles they perform are sufficiently crucial to warrant such an investment.

Another feature of linkage models is best identified in contrast to its counterpart in the other three models. In those three, the transportation and communication of knowledge proceeds primarily in one direction, the only difference being who controls the flow: practitioners in the problem-solving model, scientists and scholars in the RD&D model, and a shared responsibility in the social interaction model.

Linkage models involve a two-way knowledge *transaction* among equals in the profession rather than a knowledge transfer. They encourage a continuous flow of knowledge and allow practitioners, scientists, and scholars to lead as well as respond to practice. Indeed, the very concept of transaction includes negotiation, which accommodates the uniqueness in agencies and in the roles of practitioners.

These two distinguishing features of linkage models, combined with borrowed features from the other three models, have prompted some members of the profession to view the linkage model as the most appropriate choice (cf. Stadulis, 1973).

But the choice does remain, and it requires close evaluation of the four models' central features (presented in Table 7), including an analysis of the side effects and long-term consequences of each. The discussion to this point has been structured to enhance an understanding of the models and to suggest their possible consequences. Which model should members in the profession choose to guide their efforts?

The Communication of Knowledge

The organization, transportation, and communication of knowledge are intertwined, but they are separated here in order to focus exclusive attention on each. It should be abundantly clear by now that the organization of knowledge helps determine whether it can be communicated to just some or to all members of the profession. The models used to transport that knowledge also influence how it is communicated and by whom. For example, middle persons serve as communicators in linkage models, whereas scientists and scholars have that role in RD&D models. Nevertheless, the communication of knowledge deserves a closer look.

Table 7
Central Features of Four Models for the Transportation and Application of Knowledge

	RD&D	Social interaction	Problem-solving	Linkage
Focus	Knowledge as a product	Process of building social relations	Situation-specific needs, concerns of practitioners	Process, product, and needs, concerns of practitioners
Role of practitioner	Passive consumer of knowledge	Active partner in building relationships	Active consumer of knowledge	Active in consuming, testing, and generating knowledge
Role of scientists and scholars	Use inquiry to find goals and technologies for practitioners	Become sensitive to practitioners and help to build relationships with them	Respond to the needs, concerns of practitioners	Lead, respond as appropriate and as part of mutual, longer term pact
Flow of knowledge	One-way, as controlled by scientists and scholars	After relationships established, primarily one-way, as controlled by scientists and scholars	One-way, controlled by practitioners	Two-way, controlled jointly by researchers and practitioners
Image of exchange	Top-down transfer	Primarily a transfer	Primarily a transfer	Continuous transaction among equal colleagues

Oral Traditions

People doing all kinds of work have for ages relied more upon the spoken rather than the written word. All members of the physical education profession communicate knowledge orally, but practitioners are the most likely to do so because they do not always have time to read the latest research. Also, as already noted, the latest knowledge fails to reach some practitioners because the profession's approach to the transportation of knowledge needs improvement. Another reason for oral communication is that experiential knowledge gained by reflective inquiry usually is the subject of these conversations. This knowledge is important to practitioners, as it should be, and conversation often is the only way they can share it. Practitioners may not have the time or the inclination to formalize their thoughts into writing, and not many outlets exist for such material yet. Thus, the spoken word remains a powerful, though largely *informal*, means of communication among practitioners in the profession.

On the other hand, a profession emerges as formalized operations begin to replace informal ones. This does not suggest an end to the oral tradition in physical education, nor diminish its importance. If anything, the suggestion that greater formality is in order *adds* to the importance of informal communication. In suggesting that it needs to be formalized, we are implying that it is a valuable part of practice that may otherwise be neglected.

A profession achieves formality in two primary ways. It can use linkage models to set up formal opportunities for exchanging knowledge and skill through conversation, for example, through teacher centers, workshops, and conferences. The other way is to put conversation in writing so that experiential knowledge can reach the largest possible audience. Although oral traditions will always be important, the written word has been the most powerful in a profession such as physical education because it reaches so many members.

The Literature

As in any profession, the literature in physical education both reflects and strengthens its status. The kinds of literature available also determine to a large extent the degree and kind of communication among the field's members. Indeed the transportation of knowledge often occurs through the literature; a journal or a new book marks an effort by someone to transport and communicate knowledge to others in the profession.

The explosion of knowledge in physical education during the past three decades has seen a concomitant boom in the literature, with so much of it flooding the field that most members find it impossible to stay abreast of it all. This is especially true when international literature on physical and ludic activities is added to that from North America. For this reason, members of the profession must know what kinds of literature are available so they will know what to look for and what to expect when they find it.

Textbooks for a field serve as mini-encyclopedias, attempting to summarize the latest knowledge in the area(s) their titles identify. They can be useful for members of the profession wishing to gain literacy in a particular area of study. On the other hand, it often takes 2 years after a textbook is written for it to reach the shelves in a bookstore; it may take another 3 years before all members of the profession learn of its publication and value. Thus, by the time most persons read it, the text may already be 5 years old. In a young field such as physical education, with its rapid growth of knowledge and changes in its knowledge system, 5 years can make an incredible difference and the text may be obsolete by the time it is read. For this reason, a good text provides timeless knowledge. It gives readers literacy in an area but also directs them to periodical literature for more recent knowledge.

Journals and other periodicals differ fundamentally in the kind of knowledge they include, their intended audience, and the kind of language they use. Some present only specialized investigations, whereas others contain reviews for scientists, scholars, and practitioners. Here again, so many journals exist now that members of the profession must know what they need in order to participate efficiently in the knowledge system. Although a complete analysis of all periodical literature is inappropriate here, Table 8 lists some journals to show you the range and the kind of knowledge available.

The Future: Telecommunications and the Computer

We have recognized the importance of spoken and written words in physical education, but increasing emphasis will be given to two newer forms of communication in the future. One is through computers, and virtually everyone must gain literacy with

Table 8
Exemplary Periodicals for Physical Education

Name of periodical	Kind	Type of knowledge	Related professional association (if any)
Research Quarterly for Exercise and sport	Disciplinary and professional	Scientific	Both periodicals are published by the American Alliance for Health, Physical Education, Recreation and Dance (AAHPERD)
Journal of Physical Education and Recreation	Professional	Scholarly and experiential	
Canadian Journal of Health, Physical Education and Recreation	Professional	Scholarly and experiential	Canadian Association for Health, Physical Education, and Recreation (CAHPER)
Exercise and Sport Science Review	Disciplinary	Scientific and scholarly	
Medicine and Science in Sport and Exercise	Disciplinary	Scientific	American College of Sports Medicine Canadian Academy of Sports Medicine
Canadian Journal of Applied Sport Sciences	Disciplinary and professional	Scientific	Canadian Association of Sport Sciences
Journal of Human Movement Studies	Disciplinary	Scientific and scholarly	

Journal	Type	Orientation	Society
Journal of Biomechanics	Disciplinary	Scientific	American Society of Biomechanics Canadian Society of Biomechanics International Society of Biomechanics
Journal of Sport Psychology	Disciplinary	Primarily scientific, some scholarly knowledge	North American Society for the Psychology of Sport and Physical Activity
Journal of Motor Behavior	Disciplinary	Scientific	
Perceptual-Motor Skills	Disciplinary	Scientific	
International Journal of Sport Psychology	Disciplinary	Scientific	
Journal of Sport Behavior	Disciplinary	Scientific scholarly problems	United States Sports Academy
Review of Sport and Leisure	Disciplinary	Scientific and scholarly	
International Review of Sport Sociology	Disciplinary	Scientific and scholarly	International Committee for Sport Sociology
Journal of Sport and Social Issues	Disciplinary and professional	Scholarly	

Table 8 (Cont.)

Journal	Type	Orientation	Organization
Journal of the Philosophy of Sport	Disciplinary	Scholarly	Philosophic Society for the Study of Sport
Journal of Sport History	Disciplinary	Scholarly	North American Society for the Study of Sport History
Canadian Journal of the History of Sport and Physical Education	Disciplinary	Scholarly	
Quest	Disciplinary and professional	Scholarly	National Association for Physical Education in Higher Education
International Journal of Physical Education	Professional	Scientific and scholarly	International Committee for Health, Physical Education and Recreation (ICHPER)
Journal of Teaching Physical Education	Professional	Scientific and scholarly	
Physical Education Review	Professional	Scholarly and experiential	

The Physical Educator	Professional	Scholarly and experiential	Phi Epison Kappa (a professional fraternity)
Motor Skills: Theory in Practice	Professional	Scientific and scholarly	
Coaching Review	Professional	Scholarly and experiential	Coaching Association of Canada
Athletic Journal	Professional	Experiential	
Scholastic Coach	Professional	Experiential	
Coach and Athlete	Professional	Experiential	
The Physician and Sports Medicine	Professional	Scientific and scholarly	American Association for Fitness Directors in Business and Industry

these systems. Indeed, microcomputers already are being used in public schools, some in physical education classes. The computer opens up new possibilities for communication, storage, and retrieval of knowledge.

Telecommunication is another powerful mode of communication. Already it is possible to have closed-circuit dialogue between members of the profession worldwide as well as locally. This technology allows linkage on a grander scale than previously envisioned, knowledge that can be communicated via local, national, and international networks. These developments will usher in many changes in the way we communicate. For example the spoken word, reinforced with demonstration, can be captured on videotape; this may erode the power of the literature for some members of the profession. Please stay tuned!

Summary

The transportation and communication of knowledge are crucial to the knowledge system in physical education. Once knowledge has been generated and organized, it must be disseminated to all members of the profession if the system is to work properly. Effective functioning of the system depends in large part on the profession's approach to transporting and communicating knowledge. It is fair to state that this part of the profession's knowledge system must be improved in the future, despite the important advances of recent years.

The profession's members hold conflicting views about current approaches to the transportation and communication of knowledge, and about the roles and abilities of practitioners in the knowledge system. Although most members in the profession agree that practitioners should use new knowledge as it is generated, they disagree on whether practitioners can act on their own to stay abreast of new knowledge, and whether practitioners should generate knowledge themselves. These are crucial issues because the way they are decided determines the actions that will be taken to communicate and transport knowledge. These different actions evident in the field today reflect the conflicting views about practitioners, views involving members' perceptions about the long-term effects on practitioners of professional education and practice.

The application and transportation of knowledge can be identified in four models, with the conflicting views of practitioners spelling prominent differences in these models. Included are a research and development model, a social interaction model, a problem-solving model, and a linkage model. These are models *for* the transportation of knowledge, not *of* it. They provide some likeness of what the process might look like, and guide members of the profession as they attempt to disseminate information. The models differ considerably in what they emphasize and what they ignore. Ultimately, members of the profession must choose among them, and this requires an understanding of their features as well as their side effects. When an analysis of the four models is completed, the linkage model appears to be the superior choice because it captures the strengths of the other three, avoids their pitfalls, and adds new features that seem to facilitate the transportation of knowledge.

Although the transportation of knowledge is important, its communication is equally crucial. Interchanges among practitioners tend to be oral rather than written, and this remains viable, but the challenge in the immediate future is to establish more formal ways for these interchanges.

In this sense the field's literature is essential to communication and transportation of knowledge. Although textbooks provide a basic literacy, members of the profession will find the most up-to-date knowledge in journals. Hence, it is important to know what kinds of journals exist, who their intended audience is, and the kind of knowledge they communicate.

Computer and telecommunications systems are two other ways knowledge is communicated, with every indication that their importance will increase in the future. Members of the profession no doubt will appreciate the potential gain in literacy promised by all three forms of knowledge communication!

Supplementary Activities

Self-testing Exercises

After reading chapter 9 and reviewing its contents, you should be able to:

1. Discuss the importance of the transportation and communication of knowledge in physical education;
2. Identify conflicting views of the roles and abilities of practitioners in the knowledge system;
3. Cite examples of how conflicting views of practitioners give rise to different approaches to the transportation and communication of knowledge;
4. Identify four models for the transportation of knowledge;
5. Distinguish between the four models and make a choice among them;
6. Identify three kinds of communication in the profession and give examples of each.

Class Activities

1. Ask practitioners in various careers and agencies if new knowledge is transported to them, in understandable forms, on a regular basis. Find out how this occurs if it does, or why it does not. What consequences, if any, do practitioners see in this? Do they feel they have equal status to scientists and scholars? Pool the results in class and discuss the implications of your results.
2. Ask scientists and scholars on your faculty about their views on the roles and abilities of practitioners in physical education. Do they grant the same importance to experiential knowledge that a practitioner would? What approach do these faculty favor when the task is one of transporting and communicating knowledge? In what journals have your faculty published the results of their inquiry? What texts have they written, or helped to write? Do any serve as middle agents for a linkage model? Pool the results and discuss the similarities and differences with the results from the practitioners. What implications can be derived?

Discussion Questions

1. In your future career, do you plan to stay abreast of new knowledge as it is produced? Can you do this on your own? Do you plan to generate knowledge? If so, what kind(s)?
2. Which of the four models seems most desirable for the profession? Why? Does your answer hinge upon your future career?
3. Can practitioners be expected to read all of the journals in the

profession? Why, or why not? If not, how are they supposed to get new knowledge while it is still fresh?

4. Do practitioners on the one hand, and scientists and scholars on the other, inhabit two different worlds? Explain. What are the implications of your answer?

5. What might the future hold for the profession's modes of communication? Try to envision what might be accomplished by computers and telecommunications and share the results in class.

Sources for Additional Reading

LOCKE, L.F. From research in the disciplines to practice in the profession: One more time. *Proceedings, National Association for Physical Education in Higher Education*, 1977.

NEIL, R. Sport science magazines: A coach's guide to what's available. In N.L. Wood (Ed.), *Coaching science update, 1980-81*. Ottawa: The Coaching Association of Canada.

STADULIS, R. *Research and practice in physical education*. Champaign, IL: Human Kinetics, 1977.

CHAPTER 10
Using knowledge
in practice

We have examined the profession's approaches to generating, organizing, transporting, and communicating knowledge, and we have seen how each influences the others. Yet there remains a final and most important part of the knowledge system for physical education, and it too is affected by these other parts.

Members of the profession must put knowledge into practice, and the extent to which this occurs is a good indicator of the quality of the profession's work. This use of knowledge hinges on factors other than the knowledge system, however, and these factors will be examined in this chapter. Especially important are the type of professional education, the working environment, and the nature of the knowledge to be used. Whether these three factors ease or hinder the use of knowledge depends upon the decisions and actions of the profession's members.

The Type of Professional Education

We have documented the importance of professional education in other parts of the knowledge system for physical education, and it is equally necessary for effective knowledge use. That is, professionals cannot be expected to use knowledge if they have not received the appropriate education and training to do so. It is for this reason that so much attention has been devoted to physical education's knowledge system. Our intent is to begin providing some of this education and training. Ultimately, you should develop the commitments, understanding, and skills required for putting knowledge into practice.

A variety of methods might be used to prepare professionals for knowledge use, and for this reason professional education programs differ. These differences also are attributable to varying views on the transportation and communication of knowledge. For example, in some institutions of higher education, undergraduate students will be exposed to statistics, research design and analysis, and research-related seminars because the faculty assume that all practitioners should be able to retrieve, read, and use the results of inquiry in work.

Students in other professional education programs will examine the functions of inquiry in practice, and will be encouraged to use knowledge, but formal training and education will stop at this point. Here faculty members hold a different set of assumptions. They believe that practitioners need only acquire an appreciation for putting knowledge into practice, and that the responsibility to transport, communicate, and use the results of inquiry rests more with persons other than practitioners.

Differences such as these stem from others, as explained in previous chapters, and it is important for new members of the profession to become aware of such differences and their consequences. But if knowledge is to be put to use, the commonalities in professional education programs also should be identified.

A Common Denominator for Professional Education Programs

Despite different approaches to professional education for knowledge use, three essential outcomes may surface as a common denominator in most of our programs. At the very least, all practitioners must become *aware* of the advantages of applying new knowledge in their work and the consequences of not doing so. In addition, they must become *receptive* to the idea of altering parts of practice as new knowledge might indicate; whether the knowledge is scientific, scholarly, or experiential, it will undoubtedly suggest changes in some of the work. Receptivity is a quality beyond awareness, for it requires practitioners to step outside their immediate work roles and take an impartial look at the discrepancies between new knowledge and the way they define and perform their work at that moment.

And finally, all practitioners must gain *skills* for making necessary alterations in their work, alterations signaled by new knowledge. Whether the need is for minor improvements, major changes, or alterations in the way practice is justified, the practitioners must depart from familiar routines. Most new members in the profession are not equipped with these skills when they enter professional education; they must acquire them in these programs.

Models for Work

Perhaps the easiest way to achieve the three outcomes just described is by preparing future practitioners to design, implement, and sometimes alter their model for work. Remember, a model provides some likeness that serves to guide practitioners. It is not an exact replica, and therefore we call it a model *for*, not *of* work. It is simply an analytical device, an aid for improving work performance through knowledge use.

This point becomes clearer as we examine the process of constructing a personal model for work. Both novice and experienced practitioners who design and use such a model must give formal, systematic attention to all related parts of work as well as to the relationships among the parts. Professionals must make each facet of work explicit and testable where it might have remained unidentified and unconfirmed. In other words, models are like maps. They allow practitioners to navigate the often uncertain waters of work in an intelligent and deliberate fashion. And, like a good map, models must be tested and revised where necessary.

You can form a model for work in any career in physical education. By starting now, during your professional education, you may reap three benefits. First, you can develop early the skills to design, implement, and modify such a model. Second, you will be able to see how each of your courses relates to your future career because your model requires that these relationships be identified. Third, you will enter your first job better prepared for it because you have been directing your attention to it for 4 years.

What would such a model for work look like? Singer and Dick (1981) have provided a model for teachers of physical education, a simplified version of which is Figure 4 and which serves as an example. This systems model for teaching contains five related parts. It asks teachers to give attention to each part of work as it relates to the others, and suggests that they think about their work in a formal, systematic way rather than just "throwing out the ball" and letting students play. In identifying these five steps, Singer and Dick have assumed that students should be learning new knowledge and skills in physical education. Accordingly, they have reminded teachers to carry out parts of their work they might otherwise have neglected. The relationships among these parts have been specified, but more importantly, teachers who use this model can see how certain kinds of scientific and scholarly knowledge apply to their work.

As examples of this last point, tests for physical fitness, attitude, and skill learning can be used in step 4, the evaluation of instruction. The results from inquiry into teacher effectiveness, and the effects of different instructional styles and strategies, may apply to either step 2 (planning instruction) or step 3 (implementing instruction). Similarly, knowledge about children's growth, development, activity preferences, personal aspirations, and needs is useful in step 1, assessment. Knowledge gained from such inquiry guides the teacher in work. Singer and Dick's model thus helps you set a plan for work that you can use actively. Clearly, teachers do not always think or behave according to these steps and arrows; this is a model *for* the work involved in teaching, not *of* it.

Take another look at Figure 4 and consider a coach's work. If you substitute the coach's duties for the teacher's, and "athletes" for "students," the same model applies to coaching. Once again, the model identifies parts of coaching that might have been neglected. It also shows relationships among the different aspects of coaching and, as for teachers, suggests what kinds of knowledge apply to each duty. In both examples, a model for work serves to heighten the awareness, receptivity, and skill of practitioners in using new knowledge.

These two examples illustrate how a model for work might look, as well as some of its important functions in practice. Models may be very sophisticated, or simplified like that in Figure 4. They may frame a broad, comprehensive view of all parts of work, or they may focus on just one part of work such as the task of grading students. However complex or simple, the design and use of models should begin in professional education; indeed, the extent

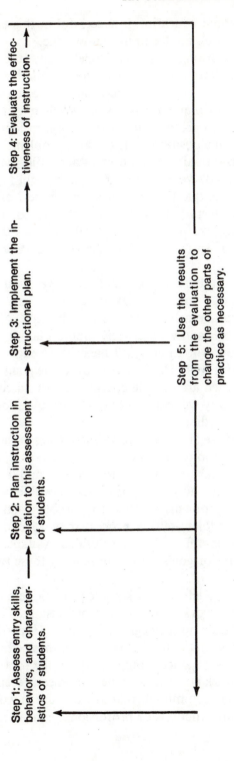

Figure 4. A simplified representation of Singer and Dick's model for teachers.

to which professional education is successful in this effort has a major impact on one's ability to use knowledge.

You can begin working on such a model at any stage in professional education. Start now by identifying a number of related questions you have, such as your goals and objectives for work: What problems do I plan to solve, what needs may I meet, and how may I help others achieve their personal aspirations? How can I ensure that I am in a position to detect such problems, needs, and aspirations? Who should decide on goals and objectives and how should they be stated? What kinds of inquiry might help me with these questions? The questions you ask, the process of answering them, and the answers you accept all are devoted to *problem-setting*. In this way you identify goals and objectives, the products of problem-setting, and they give structure to a work model for any career.

Once you have established goals and objectives, you may entertain questions about how they can be achieved and the results evaluated: How can I reach these goals and objectives? What alternatives are available, and what criteria should I adopt in choosing among them? How will I know if I have achieved my goals and performed my work well? How will I know if the goals and objectives I have identified are complete, correct, and stated properly? What kinds of inquiry will help me answer these questions and perform my work accordingly?

These questions are directed to *problem-solving* in the model for work. Whereas problem-setting yields goals and objectives, problem-solving seeks the way(s) to achieve and evaluate the former. We have seen how the approaches to problem-solving are influenced by the problems identified in problem-setting. In the same sense, the problem-setting process may depend on results from problem-solving. That is, the solutions available sometimes determine new ends or goals, thus interrelating these two parts of models for work.

To summarize, models for work guide practitioners in planning and executing their work. They remind professionals about parts of practice that should not be neglected, and they identify relationships among parts that might have gone unnoticed. They also reveal how knowledge gained from inquiry applies to work. In this way, models for work help increase the awareness, receptivity, and skill of practitioners committed to knowledge use in work. One of the most important functions of professional education is to present and emphasize models for work with future members of the profession; one of the most appropriate goals for these students is to work toward the realization of such a model and its related functions.

One final observation comes out of the relationship between professional education, knowledge use, and models for work. Preparation for the task of using knowledge in the manner we have described also provides the basis for generating knowledge. This important function is another reason your model for work should be initiated in professional education. Practitioners seeking and using knowledge in their day-to-day work will find cause to reflect upon their models, the knowledge they use, and themselves. This is the same reflective inquiry described in chapter 7, the kind of systematic, formal inquiry that generates experiential knowledge. The beauty of such experiential knowledge is that it is also generated by the most appropriate user. So, by reflecting on the new knowledge used in work, practitioners stand to generate more usable knowledge at the same time. This process thus enhances knowledge while stimulating knowledge generation.

The Conditions for Performing Work

We have seen that a professional education should prepare students to use knowledge in their work. Equally important to knowledge use, though, are the conditions surrounding the performance of work. Ideally, a direct relationship exists between the knowledge, sensitivities, and skills that result from professional preparation and the extent to which these can be used in practice. That is, in a perfect world professional education would correspond to practice.

But in our imperfect world, there often is a discrepancy between the fruits of professional education and the realities of practice. This discrepancy occurs in all professions, and relatively young professions such as physical education are especially susceptible. Aside from differences in professional education programs, the conditions surrounding work may enhance, inhibit, or prohibit the use of knowledge.

What are these conditions? Let's review some of those identified briefly in earlier chapters of Part III. Practitioners must find *time* to not only retrieve, read, and generate new knowledge, but also to reflect upon its potential use. Every professional requires such time; it makes no difference if practitioners are expected to use knowledge independently or if a middle person working in a linkage model is there to help. Knowledge use is a form of learning, and learning cannot proceed effectively unless sufficient time is devoted to it.

The *opportunity* for using knowledge is related to the time requirement. That is, the practitioner needs both formal and informal opportunities as well as those involving either a few or many peers. The use of scientific and scholarly knowledge, for example, often requires more formal opportunities, whereas the use of experiential knowledge may be enhanced by informal settings. These opportunities may be offered on the job or in gatherings such as workshops structured for knowledge sharing.

In addition, practitioners need *resources*, either human or nonhuman, if they are to use knowledge. In the first case, experts in a given area are commonly called "resource persons" because they may make the scientific, scholarly, and experiential knowledge available in usable forms. Their role is particularly significant when all three kinds of knowledge must be synthesized into a single plan or framework and applied to a specific situation. Here the resource person must possess the relevant knowledge and also must thoroughly understand the local situation. A resource person thus can facilitate the use of knowledge in situations with very specific requirements.

Nonhuman resources include the journals, books, and similar materials generated by other practitioners, as well as technologies such as computers and videotape machines. These resources must always be accessible to practitioners seeking to use knowledge.

Practitioners are encouraged to use knowledge when their efforts are *rewarded*. Although the intrinsic reward of job satisfaction comes from such utilization, knowledge is more likely to be used by everyone in the field when the agency's supervisors themselves ensure that all practitioners are rewarded for using it. Rewards may be material, but in most instances the rewards accompany personal or collective achievements and include recognition, higher status, and citations of merit. Work rewarded in this manner provides a sense of satisfaction and accomplishment because it implies performance with distinction. Knowledge use therefore will be enhanced if it is among the trademarks of distinction in work.

It was suggested in chapter 7 that knowledge yields technologies that can be readily applied to work performance, and that such technologies include new ways to teach or coach. Therefore the adoption of a new technology is a form of knowledge use, frequently requiring sustained use for its effectiveness. Consider the teacher who adopts computer-assisted instruction for the first time. This new technology changes the behaviors and expectations for teachers and students, and the teacher's professional effectiveness will likely decline when the changes are first encountered. The question is whether this decline will be temporary, and whether the teacher will continue to use the new technology (Fullan, 1982). Both cases imply the need for *follow-up assistance*, which may range from simple encouragement by peers, to on-site demonstrations, to additional education and training. With this assistance, practitioners gain confidence in themselves and the technology. Not only will their effectiveness be restored, but it is also more likely that the new technology will be used.

Finally, knowledge use demands *commitment* on the part of practitioners, and this is the most important factor of all. Professionals with this commitment are willing to put knowledge use into practice; those without it will bring little credit to themselves or their chosen career. In fact, practitioners lacking such a commitment do not merit being called professionals.

With such a commitment, conditions surrounding work performance may change over time, especially in agencies where knowledge use has been sporadic or nonexistent. A committed practitioner in that environment could become a *role-maker*, working to *create* a work situation that fosters knowledge use. Without a commitment to use knowledge, however, the practitioner in such an agency is more likely to become a *role-taker*, the result being that even the best kind of professional education will erode over the years. The point is, commitments by practitioners are the most powerful means of translating knowledge into practice.

In summary, then, some conditions in the workplace influence the extent to which knowledge is used by practitioners. These include the necessary time, opportunities, human and nonhuman resources, and follow-up assistance. Most important of all, however, are the individual and collective commitments of practitioners to utilize the knowledge. These commitments are the most important because without them practitioners cannot alter the other factors that influence the utilization of knowledge.

The discussion thus far has accentuated the positive side — showing how knowledge use can be facilitated — but these same factors under different circumstances can inhibit, if not prohibit, knowledge use. For example, many teachers also coach, and many coach more than one sport. This implies long working days, and also suggests that these teacher-coaches do not have time to incorporate new knowledge. Furthermore, they may find that physical education is isolated from the rest of the school's activities, resulting in fewer resources and no follow-up assistance. It is difficult to maintain a commitment to knowledge use under such conditions. By now it is apparent that the challenges associated with using knowledge begin in professional education but do not end there. Formidable challenges are always present in the world of practice.

The Nature of Knowledge

A third important factor in knowledge use was identified in previous chapters but merits emphasis here. The nature of the knowledge itself is a major determinant of its use, and two facets of this knowledge are especially noteworthy (Dunn, 1980).

The first has to do with how the knowledge was generated and by whom. Practitioners' use of knowledge may depend on the kind of investigations conducted, the sampling, the sources of data, and the mode of analysis. Practitioners thus may act as intelligent consumers in demonstrating their preference for certain forms of inquiry over others. In addition, because the type of inquiry is related to the persons who conduct it, practitioners may develop a preference for inquiry by scientists, scholars, practitioners, or some combination thereof. In short, the kind of inquiry and the persons who conduct it help determine whether practitioners will use knowledge.

The kind of knowledge to be used is the second consideration. That is, it makes a difference whether the knowledge is scientific, scholarly, or experiential, or for that matter whether all three kinds of knowledge can be blended together in practice. In that light, the form of the knowledge to be used may be as important as its contents, including the language used to describe it, its length and sophistication, its limitations, and whether the results can be generalized to a number of agencies and work roles within these agencies. Finally, concern about its validity and reliability reflect on the persons who generated the knowledge. All these factors help constitute the nature of knowledge and have bearing on its use in practice.

Here, too, practitioners in all professions play an active role in deciding whether to use knowledge; they can screen knowledge that will be used from that which will not, using truth, relevance, or utility tests (Weiss, 1977).

Practitioners use *truth tests* to determine if the information offered meets their personal criteria for knowledge. Whether the information is scientific, scholarly, or experiential, the practitioner applies the same truth test by asking, "Am I willing to accept this as valid knowledge?" The mode of inquiry, the person(s) who did the inquiring, the form and content of the information, and the language used to describe it all influence the outcome of truth tests, causing the information to either pass or fail.

Relevance tests may be used before, during, or after truth tests. In testing for relevance, practitioners determine how well the available knowledge fits their immediate work situation. Knowledge that passes relevance tests is more likely to be used because the practitioner sees its applicability. Knowledge that does not pass such a test probably won't be used because the practitioner reasons that it is not relevant to his or her situation, even though it may be important, and true, for others.

Relevance tests sometimes are very stringent. Without proper safeguards, they can at least limit if not prohibit the use of new knowledge, especially in those cases where practitioners have slipped into a comfortable routine. Anything departing from their routine is deemed irrelevant. However, relevance tests may be quite helpful for practitioners who understand how knowledge can be used to justify, improve, and even change practice—those who have designed a model for work and used it accordingly. With such a model, practitioners can judge more easily and effectively the future and immediate relevance of new knowledge. Without such a model, relevance tests may only reinforce existing routines, thus limiting both knowledge use and professional effectiveness.

Finally, practitioners submit knowledge to *utility tests* to find out if it really works; this is the acid test for new knowledge. If the knowledge is not useful, it usually makes little difference whether truth and relevance tests have been passed. Practitioners are by definition skilled workers in a profession and they demand results, yet the results may be direct or indirect.

Direct results are expected when the knowledge represents a new technology. For example, a teacher given new methods and a new curriculum expects these to work after a trial period; in this sense, the results are immediate and direct.

With indirect results, the new knowledge serves to *enlighten* practitioners, allowing them to see parts of their work in different ways. This understanding may not have an immediate impact upon work, but the knowledge is still useful to the practitioner. For example, a physical education teacher intent upon dramatically improving student physical fitness may learn that she has not been allotted enough time for this task; indeed, circumstances in the home and community may be eroding such efforts. Realizing this situation, the teacher has become enlightened rather than discouraged. She is then able to work to the best of her ability without questioning her own competence. In short, the knowledge gained was very useful though its results were more indirect than direct.

The fact that practitioners employ truth, relevance, and utility tests helps to emphasize the significance of the knowledge itself: The greater its integration, validity, applicability to work, and utility, the greater its use. This leads to an important conclusion. Whether we focus on professional education, the conditions surrounding work, or the nature of knowledge, persons in the profession control the extent to which new knowledge is used. Thus it is fair to conclude that knowledge use in physical education, like the entire knowledge system for the profession, is people-created and people-controlled. Any strategy for maintaining, altering, or eliminating parts of the knowledge system must therefore be directed at the profession's members.

Summary

The knowledge system for physical education is aimed at using knowledge in practice. This knowledge may result in improved practice, altered justifications for it, and occasionally more revolutionary changes affecting every aspect of practice. Related parts of the knowledge system for physical education have a major impact on whether the knowledge is used and which, if any, of these three functions are achieved. With this in mind, knowledge use cannot be viewed in a social vacuum; instead, the generation, organization, transportation, and communication of knowledge must also be considered.

Professional education is one of the three major factors influencing the use of knowledge. Unless members of the profession receive the necessary training and education to use knowledge, chances are they will not use it. Programs of professional education may vary in their approaches toward preparing future professionals for using knowledge; whichever approaches are adopted depend on the assumptions a particular faculty has accepted about the transportation and communication of knowledge.

Having granted the likelihood of such variability, three outcomes stand together as a common denominator for professional education programs. Future practitioners must gain an *awareness* of the need to use new knowledge in practice, develop some *receptivity* to its use—to the point where they learn to look for discrepancies between new knowledge and parts of practice, and master the *skills* necessary for applying knowledge to practice and making whatever adjustments this calls for.

These qualities can be facilitated by the practitioner's model for work. Models for work may be designed for any career and may range from simple representations to more complex maps of what work actually involves. Models for work usually include questions, processes, and products relating to problem-setting and problem-solving as well as the relationship between the two. These models help practitioners perform four important functions. They call attention to all relevant parts of work (some of which might have gone unnoticed), identify relationships among these parts, and help to show how new knowledge relates to work responsibilities. Models also can be vehicles for reflective inquiry; here practitioners can generate experiential knowledge at the same time and in the same place that it can be used. Thus, knowledge use is sparked by the design, implementation, and alteration of models for work in any of physical education's potential careers.

The realities of practice also determine the extent to which knowledge is used, and the practitioners' commitments to use knowledge are critical here. With such commitments, practitioners may act as role-makers to alter conditions that might temporarily inhibit or prohibit knowledge use. Knowledge use is also influenced by the time, opportunities, human and nonhuman resources, and rewards available.

Finally, the nature of the knowledge itself determines how it will be used. The type of inquiry, the persons conducting it, the kind of knowledge resulting—together with its form, content, length, validity, and reliability—all have bearing. In this regard, practitioners can be intelligent consumers of knowledge; their evaluation of it is a major factor determining whether it is used and how.

Practitioners evaluate knowledge by means of truth, relevance, and utility tests. Although knowledge can pass truth tests with some ease, relevance and utility tests are more formidable. Practitioners who have gained the awareness, receptivity, and skills for putting knowledge into practice will see more relevance and utility in new knowledge than will colleagues who do not have such a preparation for knowledge use. Here, too, models for work are valuable to committed practitioners.

Like the entire knowledge system, knowledge use is people-related and people-controlled. Therefore, attention to both must center on the profession's members beginning with you, the professional of tomorrow.

Supplementary Activities

Self-testing Exercises

After reading chapter 10 and reviewing its contents, you should be able to:

1. Explain how other parts of the knowledge system for physical education influence knowledge utilization;
2. Identify the roles of professional education, the conditions of practice, and the nature of knowledge itself in influencing knowledge utilization;
3. Discuss the unique contributions of professional education to knowledge utilization;
4. Identify the need for, and functions of, a model for work;
5. Begin to construct a personal model for work;
6. Identify the factors in practice that may facilitate, inhibit, or prohibit knowledge utilization, and indicate how they should be arranged to enhance utilization;
7. Identify characteristics of new knowledge itself that may affect knowledge utilization;
8. Identify the respective roles of truth, relevance, and utility tests in knowledge utilization, and the ways in which knowledge utilization may be enhanced in relation to them.

Class Activities

1. Survey the list of courses at your institution and determine

which are designed with an eye toward the utilization of knowledge in practice. What assumptions do they reveal about the roles of practitioners in using knowledge?

2. Simulate in class the roles of people who would welcome all kinds of new knowledge, people who might welcome some, and others who might not be interested in acquiring *any* new knowledge. Show the kinds of questions, reactions, and concerns these people might have. Then, as a class, discuss how the latter two kinds of persons might be encouraged to change their views.

Discussion Questions

1. Can practitioners demonstrate in their routines a kind of model for work, even if they are unaware of it? What are the consequences of such an inexplicit, untested model when compared to one that is explicit and tested?
2. Have you encountered examples of truth, relevance, and utility tests? Give examples.
3. Do factors other than those listed in this chapter affect the utilization of knowledge in practice? What are they? Are they more, or less, important than those already identified for you?
4. Have you already developed a commitment to use such new knowledge? Why, or why not?
5. What are the consequences for the profession itself if many of its members choose not to use new knowledge as it is produced?
6. Should scientists and scholars use the experiential knowledge that is primarily generated by practitioners? Why? How?
7. Is it desirable for all members of the profession to think of themselves as members of the same team, even though they perform different roles? Is it possible? How could you make the desirable possible?

Sources for Additional Reading

REVIEW any issue of *Motor Skills: Theory in Practice*, or, *The Coaching Review*.

ROTHSTEIN, A. Practitioners and the scholarly enterprise. *Quest*, 1973, **20**, 56-60.

ROTHSTEIN, A. (Ed.). Puzzling the role of research in practice. *Journal of Physical Education and Recreation*, 1980, **51**(2), 39-66.

CHAPTER 11
Lifelong learning: The key to professionalism

The last chapter identified factors that facilitate, inhibit, or prohibit knowledge use by practitioners. This discussion of knowledge use can now be blended with the concept of professionalism. Both the obligations of professionalism and the process of using new knowledge point in the same direction: that all in the profession must learn throughout their careers. We will examine these responsibilities for lifelong learning and identify alternative ways for this learning to occur.

Why a Concern for Lifelong Learning?

In a publication entitled *No Limits to Learning* (Botkin, Elmandjra, & Malitza, 1979), the authors identify global needs for lifelong learning. Therefore, this is an issue not just for those in physical education but for those in all professions and occupations. Acknowledging this, we will turn specifically to physical education in order to demonstrate the need for such learning.

The Shocks of the Future

If change is inevitable, as most persons would agree, then lifelong learning is essential for meeting or anticipating that change. If little learning occurs in spite of change, the result is an ever widening gap between the real world and the world as perceived by members of the profession. In the long run, this kind of gap creates unintended and unfortunate consequences in work.

For example, imagine that physical educators had not learned about women's changing roles in society and in physical and ludic activities, and had tried to limit girls and women to "ladylike" activities such as dance and archery. In so doing, these practitioners would have denied the existence of major changes in society and met with resistance from female students. This would lead to reduced effectiveness and a loss of status, both unintended and unfortunate consequences of the failure of practitioners to keep up with change by learning.

Some practitioners often are shocked at the rapid rate and content of change. Toffler (1969) calls this phenomenon future shock; it occurs when people find that the world they have believed in and been prepared for no longer exists. A prime example in any profession is when individuals receive professional education for certain programs and services and then try offering them to people long after the need for those programs has passed. Future shock can affect an entire profession, and it happens because the members have not undertaken lifelong learning.

Knowledge Obsolescence

When military equipment is no longer appropriate, military officers replace it with more suitable equipment and brand the old equipment "obsolete" because it is outdated. Members of a profession who fail to undertake lifelong learning may also become obsolete, especially those younger professions characterized by a rapid, perhaps even revolutionary, rate of knowledge production. Persons who are obsolete in the face of such knowledge are said to suffer from knowledge obsolescence. Some observers call this the new disease of professions, and it has been found to exist in physical education (Kelley & Lindsay, 1977, 1980). Naturally the practices of those persons afflicted will suffer, but there are some significant personal consequences as well. One in particular is worth mentioning because it could lead to financial disaster.

A commonly accepted legal principle is called the Doctrine of Standard Care. Applied to a professional in physical education, the principle means that the professional is ignorant in this field at his or her own peril. That is, legally one is expected to be an expert because he or she is supposed to use new knowledge and skills as quickly as they become available. When professionals fail to do so, they develop a case of knowledge obsolescence that has serious side effects. If people are injured under a professional's supervision, and the causes of the injury can be linked to the professional's failure to learn, these are legal grounds for filing suit against the professional.

Indeed, the number of court cases concerning physical education and sport has snowballed over the past 15 years, and we have every indication to believe the trend will increase. Even if the professional can muster a successful defense, the cost of these cases is considerable. A successful defense rests upon the professional's ability to demonstrate that his or her work was in keeping with the best available knowledge of the time. Consequently, where knowledge obsolescence has occurred the practitioner has little hope of preparing such a defense; the losses can be disastrous in such cases, with costs running into millions of dollars! Knowledge obsolescence is a dangerous disease that is best prevented through lifelong learning.

Burnout

Novices often enter a profession highly charged with a sense of purpose and energy. A few years later, many of them display "a progressive loss of idealism, energy, and purpose" (Edelwich & Brodsky, 1980, p. 14). That is, they are no longer motivated professionals, and the term "burnout" has been used to describe their condition. Though once oriented toward a career, burnout has reoriented them with the attitude that "a job is a job" (Edelwich & Brodsky, 1980, p. 14). Clearly, the effects on practice and the professional are negative; some persons even leave the profession because of burnout.

To prevent burnout, we must understand its causes. Among the most serious are the unrealistic expectations that new members have for the profession. The reality shocks they encounter upon entering the work world signal the beginning of burnout. Another cause is perhaps the failure of new members to pace themselves. Like runners in distance events who start too fast, new members who consume too much of their time and effort in the first few years will not be able to make a strong finish in their work. A third cause of burnout, equally serious, is that stagnation in the work-place leads to boredom and monotony, and both are enemies of learning (Houle, 1980, p. 108). Here, then, is another reason to pursue lifelong learning. It helps new members cope with change and pace themselves appropriately, and it relieves stagnation, monotony, and boredom, all of which lead to a final reason for lifelong learning.

Playful Work

Novelty is one of the most prominent attractions in any activity, including work. In its proper form and amount, novelty is stimulating and fun, enabling people to experience a kind of playfulness as they grapple with the unknown and unencountered. Novelty in work makes possible a playful attitude and contributes to the enjoyment and satisfaction people find in their work, some even going so far as to try something new just for the fun of it! For example, coaches may change their entire practice regimen because they feel the need to break from familiar routines. Teachers may allow students a new choice of activity for the same reason. In both cases, professionals and clients enjoy a change of pace that is as potentially refreshing as other forms of play.

Lifelong learning and knowledge use can be important ways of introducing novelty into the work place. Both help to make work more playful for professionals. Lest the point be missed, the enjoyment and satisfaction resulting from such work are the very ingredients that keep people attracted to it. So here are major ways to prevent burnouts and dropouts in the profession, and they also improve professional effectiveness. Like future shock, burnout, and knowledge obsolescence, playful work shows the need for concern about lifelong learning in the profession.

Having further established the need for knowledge use and life-long learning, the question now becomes "how to do it?" There are numerous ways in which members of the profession undertake lifelong learning, some already identified in previous chapters. The three most significant ways are membership in a professional association, graduate education, and learning in the workplace, all described in the remainder of this chapter.

Membership in a Professional Association

We have defined a profession as a group of people who perform a service for society, its individual members mirroring the profession just as the profession lends its identity to each member. One of the lifelines between individuals in a profession and the larger body is the professional association. Whether you plan to be a school physical education teacher, a sport manager, a physical fitness consultant, or a university professor, you can join the appropriate association(s). In fact, membership in a professional association is an obligation and it is not too soon for you to consider joining.

The value of membership in a professional association is that it keeps members in touch with new developments in the field and promotes communication with colleagues performing the same work elsewhere. After all, work can sometimes be lonely at the same time that it is rewarding, so opportunities to share ideas, approaches, and problems with colleagues are crucial. Finally, membership in a professional association reinforces one's personal identity and commitment to the profession. This is accomplished by the literature provided and by opportunities to participate in activities that shape the profession's future.

Professional associations also have other functions. They are agencies of quality control and they strive for such control in two ways. One is the process of *accreditation*, a process directed at improving the education and training of the profession's members. So when a professional association accredits an education program in a college or university, it hopes to maintain or improve the quality of the profession's members. This process is not the same as certifying the individuals who complete such a program. Such a credential or license is issued to individuals by the state or province, whereas accreditation is granted to programs, not individuals.

In order to become accredited, relevant parts of an institution of higher education must pass a thorough review by association members. Evaluated in the accreditation process are the characteristics and qualifications of faculty, the organization of individual courses and the curriculum as a whole, the quality and quantity of facilities and equipment, and the number and kind of students enrolled in the program. The rationale is that all of these relevant parts of a college or university will have an impact on the quality of students who are graduated from the institution, and that these students will in turn affect the profession as a whole. This is how the professional association provides quality control; its members thus serve as guardians of professional standards and learn from each other in the process.

Some professional associations perform another function in the name of quality control: They police the members' actions. Consequently, practitioners who do not perform their roles according to the association's expectations may be sanctioned. Sanctions range from short-term penalties to expulsion from the profession. All professional fields need these safeguards against malpractice, but few have built them into their professional associations. Physical education is among those fields without negative sanctioning for individual members. By contrast, professional associations in physical education carry many positive sanctioning mechanisms including awards and honors for members with meritorious achievements.

What are the major professional associations in physical education and kinesiology? There are too many to list here, but as you might suspect, some are primarily for practicing professionals. Regarding disciplinarians, the interdisciplinary framework for kinesiology has given rise to a number of branch associations, each bearing the name of the parent discipline. Many of these are identified in Table 8 in chapter 9. For most professionals, however, the appropriate choice of a professional association is easy. Membership in either the American Alliance for Health, Physical Education, Recreation and Dance (AAHPERD), or The Canadian Association for Health, Physical Education, and Recreation (CAHPER) is most desirable. Both organizations have student membership fees. Both send their journals and newsletters, and both provide opportunities to attend local, regional, and national conventions. In addition, membership in one association allows you to attend meetings of the other.

Thus, a professional association helps its members play an active role in the profession. It is also an important vehicle for lifelong learning through the literature it publishes, the meetings it sponsors, and the social contacts it facilitates.

Graduate Education

Some people in today's work world espouse a view of formal

education that has been called the "vaccination approach" (Postman & Weingartner, 1969). They reason that once you have completed an undergraduate degree, you have been vaccinated and become immune to the need for additional formal education. Nevertheless, graduate education is an important vehicle for lifelong learning and it also serves as a necessary prerequisite to career advancement in physical education. Since graduate education has its own set of prerequisites, it is not too early to alert you to the alternatives available.

Some graduate programs are structured toward the needs and aspirations of practitioners in a number of careers. These programs prepare students beyond the performance of current work roles; their primary focus usually is on role analysis. In short, undergraduate education focuses on role performance, whereas graduate programs prepare practitioners to analyze that role. In these graduate programs, professionals are trained and educated to become master practitioners who can perform supervisory, consultative, administrative, and coordinative roles in their work. Logically, the degree granted along these guidelines is a professional master's degree.

Of the many kinds of professional master's degrees in physical education, the most common are the master's degree in physical education (MPE) and the master's degree in education (MEd). These degrees have different goals from the programs first discussed. Here, it is assumed that the degree is the last one a person will complete. Yet this does not imply that the degree, once attained, should end all efforts to learn more. In fact, one of the objectives in many graduate programs is to prepare their degree recipients to conduct programs of lifelong learning for colleagues in the work world.

In contrast, some persons will seek a professional master's degree as a means to another end. Their master's degree is like a stop at a terminal, rather than the final degree, and their intended destination is the college or university where they will be professional faculty members. They are pursuing the doctoral degree. These degrees are commonly completed in a department of physical education, a college of education, or some combination of the two. A doctor of philosophy (PhD) or a doctor of education (EdD) degree is awarded upon completion of such study, with the assumption that these persons will have obtained some practical experience in the work world along the way. However, the primary purpose of seeking a doctoral degree is to become capable of conducting inquiry. These people are obviously important to the profession, for the field will always need researchers with appropriate background and interests. You already may be thinking about that possibility.

In addition to professional degrees, there are disciplinary degrees. The pattern for these nonprofessional options is essentially the same as that for professional ones, with the two degrees most commonly offered being master of science (MS) and master of arts (MA). These degrees may be final for some, whereas for others only the PhD will satisfy their aspirations to become scholars or faculty members. Here, too, the need exists for bright, committed people.

It should be emphasized at this point that graduate degrees, like undergraduate degrees, act as credentials. They imply what the holder is prepared to do, which of course may differ from what this individual actually does. Therefore, in one sense it makes no difference whether the degree is a PhD, an MEd, a BPE or a BEd: Every person, regardless of the degree held, carries a responsibility to engage in lifelong learning. Graduate education is a means to this end and increases each individual's responsibilities for such learning.

Learning in the Workplace

One cannot overestimate the importance of membership in a professional association and graduate education as ways to learn and to prepare for more learning. Having discussed both ways, let's look at three modes for lifelong learning in the workplace: the mode of instruction, the mode of inquiry, and the mode of performance (Houle, 1980).

The Mode of Instruction

A *mode of instruction* is the means of disseminating new knowledge, sensitivities, and skills to practitioners through direct methods such as lectures and demonstrations. Other labels describing the same process are "in-service education" and "professional development." In one sense, the mode of instruction is an attempt to bring the equivalent of graduate education into the workplace. This is surely true when outsiders give lectures and demonstrations in applying new knowledge and skills to practice.

The mode of instruction can also be used in workshops, however, where it differs from graduate education. Whereas graduate education usually focuses upon scientific and scholarly knowledge, the mode of instruction used in workshops often is based on experiential knowledge. It allows practitioners to share with peers their best tricks of the trade and the fruits of their experience. The situation is like providing the opportunity for famous chefs to swap recipes for the same gourmet meal. All such exchanges in the workplace are extremely important because scientific and scholarly knowledge are always incomplete to some extent, and because certain responsibilities in the work world demand experiential knowledge. For these reasons, practicing professionals need contact *with* each other, during which they may receive instruction *from* each other. This is an excellent way to promote learning in the workplace.

The Mode of Inquiry

The *mode of inquiry* is a second way to promote learning in the workplace. This method is employed in situations where colleagues in the profession join together to set new goals, find new ways to accomplish work, or both. In this collective endeavor, the process of exploring alternatives may be as important as the products resulting from it. Here, as in the mode of instruction, colleagues can learn from each other.

Unlike the mode of instruction, where the responsibility of helping others learn rests with only one or a few persons, the mode of inquiry is based on the assumption that all persons can contribute equally to others' learning. Whereas in the mode of instruction many of the most important products of learning can be identified in advance, this is impossible in the mode of inquiry. Indeed, if the answers were known in advance there would be no need to inquire collectively in search of them. It is in this light that the mode of inquiry's contributions are illuminated; it requires members to proceed from the known to the unknown, possibly resulting in major change.

The mode of inquiry can be used by groups of practitioners either formally or informally. It may take place at the agencies where people work, or special, adjunct agencies to the workplace may be created. The best example of the latter is the teacher center, which provides a gathering place for members in the profession. These may be open to all teachers or restricted to physical educators (Anderson, 1982). Either way, they create conditions that are ripe for the mode of inquiry, and this mode, when used successfully, is an exciting and enjoyable way to continue learning.

The Mode of Performance

A third mode of lifelong learning in the workplace is the *mode of performance*; and here the discussion will return to some familiar territory. The mode of performance begins when practitioners are able to reflect intelligently upon what they have planned, experienced, and observed. They can then use the results from this inquiry to stimulate learning. The mode of performance may be peer-directed or self-directed, and we shall look at each type.

Differences usually exist between what humans plan to do or say about themselves and how their behavior actually looks. The same is true in physical education when members of the profession sometimes engage in self-deception. If their unintended, counterproductive behaviors are to be corrected, they must first be identified, perhaps through observation by a knowledgeable peer who knows what to look for.

If the mode of performance using peer observation is to result in effective learning, then all members must have some related skills and abilities. The skills are those required for intelligent observation, whereas the related abilities are those involved with giving and receiving constructive criticism.

Several kinds of observational systems are used in physical education. Some have been applied successfully to teachers (cf. Anderson, 1980; Siedentop, 1977), and others have been developed for use by coaches (Smoll & Smith, 1980). In both systems, observation by a knowledgeable peer generates results that can be shared and discussed, an opportunity for learning by both the observer and the person observed. This peer-directed mode of performance should be used more frequently, for it leads to learning while allowing friendly and informative interaction in work, thus preventing stagnation.

The other way that the mode of performance can result in lifelong learning is through self-directed means, the best example of which is the model for work as identified in the last chapter. Not only does a model for work form the basis for systematic, reflective inquiry, but it also facilitates knowledge use and learning. As suggested previously, practitioners may reflect upon their mechanisms for problem-setting and problem-solving, generate knowledge in the process, and then learn from this knowledge. The result is meaningful learning, and its utility in the workplace can be illustrated even further.

All practitioners confront four related kinds of questions (Lawson, 1982). They confront *why* questions, *what* questions, *how* questions, and *who* questions. The collective answers to these questions can be used to form a model for work, just as reflecting on them both individually and collectively promotes learning and knowledge use. Let's look at each kind of question to illustrate this point.

Practitioners face *why* questions in two circumstances. First, they must justify their practice. For example, why should physical education be a required school subject? Why should the public be asked to support athletic programs? In the second case, practitioners ask "why" questions in trying to understand the related parts of their work. For example, why did six athletes develop muscular cramps during last Friday's basketball game? Why did the first physical education teachers believe that participation in sport built character in students? Why are some students able to learn much more quickly than others? Both kinds of "why" questions can be as useful as they are perplexing. Once raised, they cause practitioners to reflect on what they have planned, experienced, and observed. In seeking the answers, practitioners are bound to learn.

For instance, in trying to justify a required program of physical education, the results of the latest inquiry into their effectiveness would have to be reviewed. The same holds true when justifying athletic programs. Furthermore, in seeking answers to the question about muscular cramps, practitioners would have to consult the literature on motor control. They would find reminders and new information about fluid replacement during competition, the effects of relative humidity, temperature, and altitude, and the role of fatigue.

In exploring why people thought sport builds character, they would read the latest findings on psychosocial outcomes from sport participation, and trace the evolution of this belief back to the previous century in Victorian England. In trying to understand why differences occurred in the amount students learned, the teacher would have to consider the latest findings on the relationship between teaching strategies and learning styles, the way in which the content was organized and presented, and the most up-to-date information about teacher effectiveness. These examples all reveal how learning and knowledge use can result from reflecting on two kinds of "why" questions.

"Why" questions may be pursued for their own sake as a means of satisfying personal curiosity. However, "why" questions of the second kind often lead to "what" and "how" questions. In other words, questions in the mode of performance are as interrelated as the parts of work themselves.

With "what" questions, the practitioner must consider the relationship between current and future states of work. By looking at work and its outcomes today, an understanding of what should be done tomorrow often emerges. This understanding produces goals and objectives, which point toward what practitioners hope to accomplish for society in the future. "What" questions provide a basis for problem-setting, by which practitioners may engage in learning and knowledge use as they reflect on the problems they plan to identify.

For example, what achievements mark the physically educated student? What goals are appropriate for school athletic programs? These questions lead back to "why" questions. Why were programs of physical education and athletics established in the first place? Are the same factors responsible for their current design and conduct? Why have programs been justified differently in other historical periods? The literature in sport studies would have to be consulted concerning these "what" and "why" questions. At the same time, however, the literature can only suggest what was or is the case in relation to these programs. Their ideal goals cannot be derived from the literature alone, but are formed by personal and collective value judgments. Thus, reflecting on "what" questions can result in knowledge use from sport studies, but an equally important outcome is that of identifying and learning about personal and professional values. In both cases, significant kinds of learning may result from the mode of performance.

"Why" and "what" questions together lead to *how* questions. "How" or "how best" questions concern the choice of methods for accomplishing goals. In other words, these questions highlight the ways practitioners try to solve problems, not set them. For example, how best can we make fourth-grade children physically fit? How best can tennis be taught to senior citizens? "How" questions are crucial in work, and reflecting upon them demands a look into the literature while examining personal performance as well.

Furthermore, an understanding of the "why" questions involved makes answering "how" questions much easier. For example, learning why children become physically fit under some circumstances and not others eases the task of deciding how to make a class more fit. Similarly, an understanding of why senior citizens require special approaches to learning, special adaptations of sports, and special equipment makes it easier to decide how to teach them tennis.

Thus, any choice of methods and the reflection on these choices requires a blend of experiential, scientific, and scholarly knowledge. It is also in connection with "how" questions that knowledge is generated as it is used, clearly an important form of learning through the mode of performance.

Finally, "what" and "how" questions are related to "who" questions, which raise the issue about the dynamics of decision-making in work. Who should make decisions about what parts of work? Should students in schools be allowed to participate in decisions about what they should learn and how? Should athletes help decide a starting lineup for the next contest? Should a supervisor make all the decisions regarding allocation of funds for the department? These kinds of "who" questions may also be sources for reflective inquiry.

Like the other three kinds of questions, the literature should be consulted—in this case perhaps literature on group dynamics, on models for administrative decision-making and leadership, and on personalized learning. Like the other kinds of questions, the practitioners also could examine personal and professional values as well as the fruits from past experience. Here is another opportunity for learning through reflective inquiry. Moreover, if "who" questions broaden the opportunities to participate in decision-making, then learning itself will be enhanced by the new forms of interaction it allows practitioners. Such a cascade effect often results from a professional's efforts to learn, especially when it proceeds through the mode of performance.

To summarize, practitioners learn by considering each of the four kinds of questions, which often are interrelated, as shown in

Table 9. Learning in connection with one therefore often prompts learning with the others. Furthermore, each question is related to parts of the profession's subject matter, as shown in Tables 9 and 10.

Thus, the mode of performance is an important way to continue lifelong learning and to use knowledge. Whether peer-directed or self-directed, it produces meaningful results in usable forms. Reflection about why, what, how, and who questions triggers an important mixture of scientific, scholarly, and experiential knowledge that together forms a model for work. This, then, is a powerful tool for improving practice and learning from it.

Summary

In some ways a profession is like a chain in that the whole is only as strong as its weakest link. This observation points to the fact that physical education will gain more importance as a profession through the actions of its individual members, the most significant of which is lifelong learning by each member. An efficient knowledge system is but one step in this direction.

The lack of effective approaches to lifelong learning can cause members to experience future shock, knowledge obsolescence, and burnout. When these states occur in individual members of the profession, not only is their effectiveness reduced but also the effectiveness of the profession as a whole. The value of ongoing learning in preventing these conditions cannot be overlooked. Moreover, this learning can elicit playful approaches to work, which in turn can improve professional effectiveness. Thus, these are good reasons for directing attention toward lifelong learning.

Among the many possible approaches to this learning, three are especially important. One of these is membership in a professional association, which provides a direct line of communication with other members of the profession through literature, meetings, and social contacts — all important stimuli for learning. Graduate education is another way to continue one's learning. And it can allow persons to assume the responsibility for generating continued learning in their colleagues.

However, the third and most important way to engage in learning is to build it into the workplace, using any of three modes: the mode of instruction, the mode of inquiry, and the mode of perfor-

Table 9

An Example of the Relationships Between the Four Kinds of Questions

Why questions	What questions	How questions	Who questions
Why was physical education added to the school's curriculum?	What is the subject matter of physical education?	How should teachers organize their curricula?	Who should make curricular decisions?
Why should physical education be required of all students?	What goals mark the physically educated student?	How should they teach?	Who should decide the basis for grading students?

Table 10
The Kinds of Questions and Their Related Subject Matter

Kind of question	Related subject matter
"Why" (scientific/scholarly)	Motor control
	Sport studies
"Why" (justification)	Sport studies
	Sport pedagogy
"What"	Sport studies
	Sport pedagogy
"How"	Sport pedagogy
	Motor control
"Who"	Sport studies
	Sport pedagogy

mance. All three are effective and merit the attention of the profession's members. These modes should promote knowledge use and learning in the profession, which will elevate the profession's status, the services it offers to society, and each member's feelings of self-worth.

Supplementary Activities

Self-testing Exercises

After reading chapter 11 and reviewing its contents, you should be able to:

1. Define future shock, knowledge obsolescence, and burnout. Indicate how continuing learning can prevent their occurrence;
2. Identify the functions of a professional association, the advantages of membership in one, and the ways in which this membership can facilitate continuing learning;
3. Identify the kinds of advanced degrees to be gained through graduate study in physical education;
4. Distinguish between the mode of instruction, the mode of performance, and the mode of inquiry by citing examples of each;
5. Discuss the relationship between why, what, how, and who

questions and give examples of how they may facilitate knowledge use and continuing learning.

Class Activities

1. In a class discussion, list the kinds of careers that students plan
   to enter, and then show how continuing learning and knowledge use may be facilitated in each. Do certain ways work well
   for every career? How do you know? Why might some ways
   work well with one career and not with others? What might the
   future hold in this regard?
2. Interview practitioners in these careers to get their views on continuing learning, use of knowledge, and the ways in which both
   may be accomplished.

Questions for Discussion

1. What are some of the why, what, how, and who questions you
   may expect to confront in your career? For now, what answers
   would you give for each? Are your answers, when taken together, consistent and useful?
2. Is graduate education a requirement for your career?
   Desirable? How do you know?
3. Do you undertake continuing learning other than through formal classes? How? Would these methods work well in your
   future career?
4. Do people drop out of the profession because they burn out,
   or are there other reasons? If so, what are these? Can they be
   prevented? Is continuing to learn a help?
5. Is knowledge obsolescence possible in your intended career?
   How would you know if it had occurred?
6. Identify ways in which your future work can be made more
   playful.
7. What observational systems are available for your intended
   career? Do they allow you to focus upon all of the relevant
   parts of this work?
8. What are the legal responsibilities of persons in your intended
   career?
9. Which periodicals appear to offer knowledge and skills that
   apply most immediately and directly to your intended career?
10. What mechanisms for quality control exist in your intended

career? What additional mechanisms might be necessary in the near future?

Sources for Additional Reading

ANDERSON, W.G. A physical education program development center. *Journal of Physical Education, Recreation and Dance,* 1982, 53(5), 7; 9-10.

ARGYRIS, C., & Schon, D. *Organizational learning: A theory of action perspective.* Reading, MA: Addison-Wesley, 1978.

CRASE, D., & Sachs, M. Information retrieval systems for professionals in physical education and sport. *Journal of Physical Education and Recreation,* 1980, 51(2), 65-66.

EARLS, N.F. How teachers avoid burn-out. *Journal of Physical Education, Recreation and Dance,* 1981, 52(9), 39-40.

JENSEN, M. Teaching as an open skill. *Quest,* 1980, **32**(1), 60-70.

LAWSON, H.A. A conceptual model for the application of sport studies to practice. *Motor Skills: Theory in Practice,* 1982, 5(1).

PART 4

An introduction to the profession of physical education must entice its prospective members to think about the future, and this is the intent of chapter 12. The discussion is not lengthy, but it does include related challenges associated with the future. The intent is to make readers think about the ways in which they may actively *create* a desirable future, rather than just respond to changes over which they have little control. Preparation for this more appropriate, active role in shaping the future of the profession begins now with adequate analysis of the profession's potential for meeting these challenges and others that readers themselves are better equipped to identify.

CHAPTER 12
Challenges of the
21st century

Today's introductory students in physical education will remain active, working members of the profession well into the 21st century. Recognition of this fact ushers in a futuristic perspective, inviting all members of the profession to imagine what work will be like in the next century. It also should encourage you to think about ways you can prepare now in order to meet future challenges. Although this process is difficult, it gets easier if you think of it as a kind of futures forecasting. A forecast requires you, the futurist, to make some reasoned predictions. These predictions can be of two kinds, their major difference being in the way you derive them.

Normative predictions, like normative inquiry, reflect the values or standards of the futurist. They suggest either directly or by implication what things should look like in the future, even though this picture may differ dramatically from existing conditions. Indeed, values or standards in a futurist's predictions are best detected when you discover a gap between the world of today and the proposed world of tomorrow.

Although the predictions may reflect the futurist's personal values, nevertheless they are immensely valuable. Consider that tomorrow's world begins with the ideas of today, and the imagination and values of a good futurist can suggest to members of the profession the kind of world they should work to *create*. Indeed, futurists who make normative predictions often begin by analyzing current affairs and identifying what is undesirable, then offering a predictive framework designed to improve human life.

The second kind of prediction also begins with an analysis of today's world, and in this sense the predictions are grounded in reality. In *grounded predictions*, the futurist identifies current trends and then makes reasoned judgments about whether these trends will persist into the future. The intent is to describe, more than prescribe. These predictions demand a special understanding of society in both historical and contemporary perspectives, because only with such an understanding is it possible to make a reasoned judgment about the probable persistence of today's trends and conditions. In short, grounded predictions are products of extrapolation, not crystal-ball gazing.

Although normative and grounded predictions differ, they are similar in the sense that grounded predictions may portray a future for the profession that appears undesirable to its members. With this negative scenario in mind, however, they can make normative predictions designed to produce a more desirable state of affairs. Here is another similarity between the two kinds of predictions: Both require personal and professional evaluation of their contents, and both demand personal and professional action in relation to them. This action may be to speed toward the future on the present course, or to redirect the course of the future. Whatever the intent, active—not passive—responses must characterize members in a profession. Even a meager understanding of history testifies that people have changed its course, and that no prediction is "chipped into stone."

The remainder of the discussion is built on the preceding framework. We have identified challenges that might also serve as predictions, some normative, others grounded. It is important to detect both kinds and evaluate each accordingly because both kinds of challenges invite you to contemplate the personal and professional actions being taken today. Indeed, your actions may include preparing for these challenges as well as working to speed or to arrest their effects. Finally, your actions may involve identifying additional challenges, perhaps even designing a future scenario for the profession.

What, then, are some of the challenges of the next century? This chapter will suggest nine of them and comment briefly on each.

Improving the Physical Educator's Image

The first challenge is already being accepted by many in the profession today, but you also must plan on meeting it because this takes time. To many, physical educators represent only the body, not the mind. This "dumb jock" stereotype is very old and should be put to rest. The image of the physical educator merits a more accurate portrayal.

You can help put an end to this negative stereotype by learning to think and speak as skillfully as you now perform in physical and ludic activities. If you commit yourself to this goal, your liberal and professional education will enable you to meet this challenge successfully.

Improving Physical Education Programs

The second challenge, both familiar and enduring, is that of improving the content and conduct of school physical education programs. Although this task has occupied members of the profession for most of the 20th century, a great deal of work remains to be accomplished. For example, some schools still employ individuals to teach physical education whose only qualifications include past experiences as a performer or little league coach. And students in some classes are not required to learn the subject matter of physical education, but instead are allowed to play whatever game is in season, even though these same games were offered during the same seasons for the preceding 5 years!

Perhaps most significant is that programs for elementary school students, complete with specialized or highly competent teachers, are rare—despite overwhelming evidence citing the importance of appropriate experiences during childhood. These are just a few examples indicating the need for improvement in current school programs. They challenge members of the profession to improve the content and conduct of school physical education programs and, as a result, to enhance the quality of life for everyone.

Improving Athletic Programs

The third challenge is to improve school, college, and university athletic programs. Although these programs have been visible and effective in the past, the spiraling costs associated with athletics today suggest that their future is cloudy unless program organizers can find new funding sources. Another point is that despite statements to the contrary, athletic programs have not been available to everyone. Instead, teams have been trimmed to accommodate only the best athletes, overlooking less skilled children whose parents also pay taxes. "Sport for all" has been an enduring justification for these programs, but that slogan should become a reality. Still, expanded participation means even greater costs.

Furthermore, improvements in athletic programs must include increased recognition for athletes' rights on at least two fronts. Athletes must receive the education they merit, or have been promised, rather than being exploited in an athletic system. In addition, athletes in schools should not be trapped between sport programs in the community and those in the school; organizers for both kinds of sport programs must cooperate in the athletes' behalf.

Second, the qualifications of coaches must be improved—a measure that should improve the quality of athletic programs as well. Coaching effectiveness and certification programs already are available in the United States and Canada, so the future of athletics appears promising if members of the profession will only take the initiative.

Integrating School and Community Programs

A fourth challenge, related to the previous two, comes out of the redefinition for the profession of physical education. Though once limited exclusively to teacher-coaches who worked in schools, colleges, and universities, membership in the profession now includes persons who work in numerous other agencies. Furthermore, earlier 20th century school physical education and athletic programs were largely unique in offering instructional, participatory, and competitive opportunities in physical and ludic activities. That is no longer true, and the future promises even greater differences. In one sense, this observation alone suggests the need to improve the content and conduct of school programs and make them unique again.

In another sense, however, members of the profession face the greater challenge of integrating the people and programs of educational institutions and community agencies. That is, they must ensure that one group's offerings complement those of another group, a challenge that requires immediate planning. Professional preparation programs must be integrated, and cooperative ventures between educators and people in the community must be explored. Clearly, people deserve such programs and services throughout their lives, and it is up to members in the profession to plan accordingly.

Promoting Better Understanding of Performance

A fifth challenge is to increase people's understanding of the dimensions and importance of their involvement in physical and ludic activities. To be sure, people understand it better today than in the past but this is still not enough. For example, those seeking improved health need to know more about principles of training and conditioning in order to be certain they are choosing the right kind and amount of activity.

On the other hand, many persons see performance only in instrumental terms. They want to become more physically fit, earn an athletic scholarship, or find a release for tension. Such instrumental thinking is commendable of course, since these reasons all contribute to improvements in lifestyle. Yet, there are other dimensions associated with performance, and an understanding of them would accomplish two worthy goals: The amount of participation would increase and the status of physical educators would be upgraded as well.

Foremost among these dimensions is the promotion of performance as art and expression. Achieving this goal requires greater emphasis on the art of performing and on physical and ludic activities as performing arts. These dimensions of performance are uniquely human qualities that elevate human performance above that of animals. Athletes, like dancers, should not be described in animalistic terms; they create beauty, and the challenge of getting society to understand and appreciate this is an important one in the years ahead.

Protecting Human Involvements in Ludic Activities

A sixth challenge, as already identified in an earlier chapter, is to protect human involvement in ludic activities, particularly in sport. This parallels the challenge of promoting and encouraging participation, but it also differs. For example, consider the sport involvement of preadolescent children. All such participation is not necessarily beneficial for them, at least not the way programs currently are designed and conducted. Although some sport experiences may offer worthy developmental and educational benefits, commercialism and professionalism often intrude, eroding not only the benefits but also the reasons for participating. Consequently, many children may turn away from sport.

In a commercialized and professionalized approach to ludic activities such as sport, participation is viewed as a privilege. But an educational and developmental approach views participation as a *right*! And, like other rights, the right to involvement in ludic activities often is endangered by forces such as commercialism, professionalism, sexism, and racism, and by those who choose to exploit the participation of others. In the face of these threats, physical educators must act like lawyers in promoting and defending the peoples' right to participate, be they children or adults, males or females.

Using Available Technologies

Technology in the broadest sense refers to the organization of knowledge for achievement of practical purposes. Another challenge for the profession, then, is to use all such technologies that become available. It especially behooves us to use machine technologies such as the microcomputer and other computerized operations that have remarkable abilities to receive, store, retrieve, and communicate information. For example, a new machine for exercise prescription soon will be available. After users receive initial counseling, the machine is programmed accordingly so they simply key in an identification code each time they enter the facility. The machine can talk to people reminding them about the previous exercises they attempted and suggesting what they should try today. This machine is just one example of the many exciting technologies that are becoming available. Others include three-dimensional representations of skilled performance in all kinds of activities (quite a teaching aid!) and computer-assisted decision-making technologies for coaches in all sports.

Although we should always question the desirability of a technology, members of the profession should embrace appropriate technologies rather than avoid them. These technologies must be understood, their requirements mastered, and then used properly. Far from eliminating the need for professionals, most such technologies create an even greater demand for them; the task is to recast the roles of professionals in relation to new technology. In other words, the challenge is not only to change with the times but also with the technologies.

Improving the Working Conditions for Members in the Profession

An eighth challenge, focusing on the health and welfare of members in the physical education profession, is to improve working conditions in the various careers members can select. Although some of these conditions will improve as the knowledge system for the field grows, it will take further action to fully meet this challenge.

Members of the profession have always been distinguished by their commitment and sincerity. They have worked long hours, often with minimal or no pay, for the duties they have accepted. Think about the average school teacher in this connection, or the coach. The hours they donate as part of their labor of love often are beyond calculation. Although these attitudes are commendable and hopefully will remain intact in the future, the situation also causes alarm. Over the years, the demands of work can exact a terrible toll on workers in the profession; many leave the field, whereas others who remain become tired to the point of "burnout." In either instance, the quality of work in the profession suffers. That is, a person's work should improve with age and experience, but as people leave the profession they often are replaced by novices. This creates an imbalance in seasoned versus rookie professionals. Moreover, when people become tired they cannot engage in life-long learning, or they do not find the time and effort to devote to programmatic and personal change; again the quality of work and life is reduced.

Physical educators and recreationists are not alone in confronting problems in their working conditions, of course, but there is a touch of irony here: Both professional groups have endeavored over the years to "re-create" people for the demands of their work. They have suggested that people go for a run, take a swim, or play tennis to escape and compensate for conditions and demands of their work. Now many of the same problems exist in their own work; should they, too, try to compensate by exercising when that activity is already a part of their work? The answer is apparent. The actual working conditions must be changed and members in the profession are responsible for working toward their own betterment in this regard. By striving to meet this challenge now, physical educators and recreationists can create the profession's future.

Fostering International Understanding

The last challenge suggested for members of the profession is to expand current efforts to meet their responsibilities as professionals and citizens on a shrinking planet. Although nationalism probably will continue for some time, it is also possible to envision participation in a world community. Indeed, some of the problems and challenges in the North American physical education profession are also those shared by colleagues around the world.

Humans around the world participate in forms of physical and ludic activities. This involvement clearly attests to our common humanity and also holds the potential of uniting us in the name of mutual understanding and cooperation. We have made a beginning with international competition in highly competitive sports, (telecommunications can enhance this internationalsim), but the surface has hardly been scratched. Members of the profession can play a major part in creating a world community, thereby enhancing the quality of life. Surely this is the most pressing challenge of all!

Summary

Both new and experienced members in the profession should look to the future with hope, optimism, and a commitment to action. This future may be *forecasted* using normative and grounded predictions, but it is *created* by the actions of members in the profession. Therefore, professionals must take an active role with such predictions rather than remain passive with the assumption that one future is more inevitable than others. History reveals that events unfold in relation to people's actions as well as their inactions, and the same is true in physical education.

Members of the physical education profession will encounter numerous challenges in the next century. Of these, nine examples were suggested that could double as grounded and normative predictions: improving the physical educator's image, improving school physical education programs, improving athletic programs, integrating school and community programs, promoting a better understanding of performance, protecting human involvement in ludic activities, using available technologies, improving the working conditions for members in the profession, and fostering international understanding. No doubt other challenges exist as well, and the task of identifying and meeting them rests with all members of the profession.

It is difficult to think about and predict the future, let alone to plan and act in relation to such thoughts. Yet it must be done, as the following Greek legend illustrates.

Two brothers, Prometheus and Epimetheus, faced life on quite different terms, despite the fact that the two had been raised identically. Prometheus was a master of wise forethought. He always seemed to know in advance what was going to happen, when, and why, and as a consequence he could *act* in anticipation of events. This ability to anticipate allowed him to use these events to his own best advantage. His brother Epimetheus, by contrast, was not so farsighted. Because he was oriented only toward the past and present, new events always took him by surprise. He was so busy trying to understand what had happened and why, that his only alternative was to *react* afterward. Therefore he was always at a disadvantage in dealing with the problems of life, ill-prepared as he was to see over the horizon.

Thus, the most fitting and concluding question for members of the profession would be: Do you intend to fit the mold of Epimetheus, forever reacting and wondering why, or will you become one of the New Prometheans?

REFERENCE NOTES

1. Sparks, R.E.C. The educational value of high risk sports in the physical education program. Paper presented at the AAHPERD National Convention, Houston, TX, April 1982.
2. Kretchmar, R.S. Bodily skill and liberal education. Unpublished manuscript, State University College at Brockport, NY, 1979.

REFERENCES

ABERNATHY, R., & Waltz, M. Toward a discipline: First steps first. *Quest*, 1964, **2**, 1-7.

ANDERSON, W.G. *Analysis of teaching physical education*. St. Louis: C.V. Mosby, 1980.

ANDERSON, W.G. A physical education development center. *Journal of Physical Education, Recreation, and Dance*, 1982, **53**(5), 7; 9-10.

ARGYRIS, C., & Schon, D. *Organizational learning: A theory of action perspective*. Reading, MA: Addison-Wesley, 1978.

AVEDON, E.M., & Sutton-Smith, B. *The study of games*. New York: J. Wiley, 1971.

BAIN, L.L. Perceived characteristics of selected movement activities. *Research Quarterly*, 1979, **50**(4), 565-573.

BERRYMAN, J. From the cradle to the playing field: America's emphasis on highly organized competitive sports for preadolescent boys. *Journal of Sport History*, 1975, **2**(1), 115-131.

BLEDSTEIN, B.J. *The culture of professionalism: The middle class and the development of higher education in America*. New York: W.W. Norton, 1976.

BOTKIN, J.W., Elmandjra, M., & Malitza, M. *No limits to learning: Bridging the human gap*. Toronto: Pergamon, 1979.

BRESSAN, E. 2001: The profession is dead—Was it murder or suicide? *Quest*, 1979, **31**(1), 77-82.

BROEKHOFF, J. Physical education as a profession. *Quest*, 1979, **31**(2), 244-254.

BROEKHOFF, J. A discipline—So who needs it? *Proceedings, National Association for Physical Education in Higher Education*. Champaign, IL: Human Kinetics, 1982.

BROHM, J.M. *Sport: A prison of measured time*. London: Ink Links, 1978.

BRONSON, A.O. *Clark W. Hetherington: Scientist and philosopher*. Salt Lake City: University of Utah Press, 1958.

CAILLOIS, R. *Man, play, and games*. New York: Free Press of Glencoe, 1961.

CAPLAN, N. The two communities theory and knowledge utilization. *American Behavioral Scientist*, 1973, **22**(3), 459-470.

CONANT, J.B. *The education of American teachers*. New York: McGraw-Hill, 1963.

DRESSEL, P.L. Liberal education: Developing the characteristics of a liberally educated person. *Liberal Education*, 1979, **6**, 315-322.

DUNN, W.E. The two communities metaphor and models of knowledge use: An exploratory case study. *Knowledge: Creation, Diffusion, Utilization*, 1980, **1**(4), 515-536.

EARLS, N.F. How teachers avoid burn-out. *Journal of Physical Education, Recreation, and Dance*, 1981, **52**(9), 39-40.

EDELWICH, J., & Brodsky, A. *Burn-out in the helping professions.* New York: Human Sciences, 1980.

ETZIONI, A. *The semi-professions and their prospects.* New York: Free Press, 1969.

FULLAN, M. *The challenge of educational change.* New York: Teachers College Press, 1982.

GLAZER, N. The schools of the minor professions. *Minerva,* 1974, **12**(3), 346-364.

GRUNEAU, R.S. Freedom and constraint: The paradoxes of play, games, and sport. *Journal of Sport History,* 1981, **7**(3), 68-86.

HAAG, H. (Ed.). *Sport pedagogy.* Baltimore: University Park Press, 1978.

HARPER, W. Movement and measurement: The case of the incompatible marriage. *Quest,* 1973, **20**, 92-98.

HARPER, W. Literature: A messenger of truth. *Journal of Physical Education, Recreation, and Dance,* 1982, **53**(2), 37-39.

HAUG, M. The deprofessionalization of everyone? *Sociological Focus,* 1975, **8**, 197-213.

HAVELOCK, R. *A guide to innovation in education.* Ann Arbor, MI: Institute for Social Research, 1969.

HENRY, F.M. Physical education: An academic discipline. *Journal of Health, Physical Education, and Recreation,* 1964, **35**, 32-33; 69.

HENRY, F.M. The academic discipline of physical education, *Quest,* 1978, **29**, 13-29.

HOULE, C. *Continuing learning in the professions.* San Francisco: Jossey-Bass, 1980.

HOUSE, E.R. Technology vs. craft: A ten year perspective on innovation. *Journal of Curriculum Studies,* 1979, **11**(1), 1-15.

HUIZINGA, J. *Homo ludens: A study of the play element in culture.* Boston: Beacon, 1955.

INGHAM, A.G. Occupational sub-cultures in the work world of sport. In J. Loy & D. Ball (Eds.), *Sport and social order.* Reading, MA: Addison-Wesley, 1976.

KELLEY, E., & Lindsay, C. Knowledge obsolescence in physical educators. *Research Quarterly,* 1977, **48**(2), 463-474.

KELLEY, E., & Lindsay, C. A comparison of knowledge obsolescence of graduating seniors and practitioners in the field of physical education. *Research Quarterly for Exercise and Sport*, 1980, **51**(4), 636-644.

KENYON, G.S. A conceptual model for characterizing physical activity. *Research Quarterly*, 1968, **39**, 96-105.

KLEINMAN, S. Philosophy and physical education. In R. Singer (Ed.), *Physical education: An interdisciplinary approach*. New York: MacMillan, 1972.

KROLL, W. *Perspectives in physical education*. New York: Academic Press, 1971.

LAMB, D.R. Physiology and physical education. In R. Singer (Ed.), *Physical education: An interdisciplinary approach*. New York: MacMillan, 1972.

LARSON, L.S. Professional preparation for the activity sciences. *Journal of Sports Medicine*, 1965, **5**, 15-22.

LAWSON, H.A. A conceptual model for the application of sport studies to practice. *Motor Skills: Theory in Practice*, 1982, **5**(1).

LAWSON, H.A., & Morford, W.R. The cross-disciplinary nature of kinesiology and sport studies: Distinctions, complications, and advantages. *Quest*, 1979, **31**(2), 231-243.

LAWSON, H.A., & Pugh, D.L. Six significant questions about performance and performance courses in the major. *Journal of Physical Education and Recreation*, 1981, **52**(3), 59-61.

LEWIS, G. Adoption of the sports program, 1906-1939: The role of accommodation in the transformation of physical education. *Quest*, 1969, **12**, 34-46.

LOCKE, L.F. Introduction. *Quest*, 1972, **18**, 1.

LOCKE, L.F. From research and the disciplines to practice and the profession: One more time. *Proceedings of the NCPEAM/NAPECW National Conference*, 1977, pp. 34-45.

LOY, J.W. Sociology and physical education. In R. Singer (Ed.), *Physical education: An interdisciplinary approach*. New York: MacMillan, 1972.

MAHEU, R. Sport and culture. *International Journal of Adult and Youth Education*, 1962, **14**, 169-178.

McCAIN, G., & Segal, E. *The game of science*. Monterey, CA: Brooks/Cole, 1973.

MORFORD, W.R. Toward a profession, not a craft. *Quest*, 1972, **18**, 88-93.

MORFORD, W.R., & Lawson, H.A. A liberal education through the study of human movement. In W. Considine (Ed.), *Alternative professional preparation in physical education*. Washington: AAHPERD, 1978.

MORFORD, W.R., Lawson, H.A., & Hutton, R.S. A crossdisciplinary model for undergraduate education. In H.A. Lawson (Ed.), *Undergraduate education: Issues and approaches*. Washington, DC: AAHPERD, 1981.

POSTMAN, N., & Weingartner, C. *Teaching as a subversive activity*. New York: Dell, 1969.

RAINWATER, C. *The play movement in the United States: A study of community recreation*. Chicago: University of Chicago Press, 1922.

ROTHMAN, J. *Using research in organizations*. Beverly Hills, CA: Sage, 1980.

ROTHSTEIN, A. Practitioners and the scholarly enterprise. *Quest*, 1973, **20**, 56-59.

ROTHSTEIN, A. Puzzling the role of research in practice. *Journal of Physical Education and Recreation*, February 1980, pp. 39-40.

SHEEHAN, T. Sport: The focal point of physical education. *Quest*, 1968, **10**, 59-67.

SIEDENTOP, D. *Developing teaching skills in physical education*. Boston: Houghton-Mifflin, 1977.

SINGER, R., & Dick, W. *Teaching physical education: A systems approach*. Boston: Houghton-Mifflin, 1981.

SMOLL, F.L., & Smith, R.E. Techniques for improving the self-awareness of youth sports coaches. *Journal of Physical Education, Recreation, and Dance*, 1980, **51**(2), 46-48.

STADULIS, R.E. Bridging the gap: A lifetime of waiting and doing. *Quest*, 1973, **20**, 47-53.

STADULIS, R.E. *Research and practice in physical education*. Champaign, IL: Human Kinetics, 1977.

STILES, L.J. Liberal education and the professions. *Journal of General Education*, 1974, **26**(1), 53-64.

TOFFLER, A. *Future shock*. New York: Bantam, 1969.

TOREN, N. Deprofessionalization and its sources. *Sociology of Work and Occupations*, 1975, **2**, 323-337.

WEISS, C. *Using social research in public policy making.* Lexington, MA: D.C. Heath, 1977.

WESTON, A. *The making of American physical education.* New York: Appleton-Century-Crofts, 1962.

INDEX